HOME ELECTRICS

WIRING AND MAINTENANCE

HOME ELECTRICS

WIRING AND MAINTENANCE

by Julian Worthington
and David Knight

AURA BOOKS
London

This limp edition published 1984
by Aura Book Distribution Limited
2 Derby Road, Greenford, Middlesex

in association with
W. Foulsham & Company Limited
Yeovil Road, Slough, Berkshire, SL1 4JH

We should like to thank M.K. Electric Ltd. for supplying some of the equipment used to illustrate this book.

ISBN 0-572-01268-3

Photoset in Great Britain by Rowland Phototypesetting Ltd., Bury St Edmunds, Suffolk and printed in Hong Kong

Maintenance Repairs

The following symbols have been included to provide you with instant help when confronted with future routine repairs. If you look at the fore-edge of the book you will notice that some of the pages show black ink on the trim. These are the pages on which you will find our Symbols and in which you will find D.I.Y. instruction on the repairs which they represent.

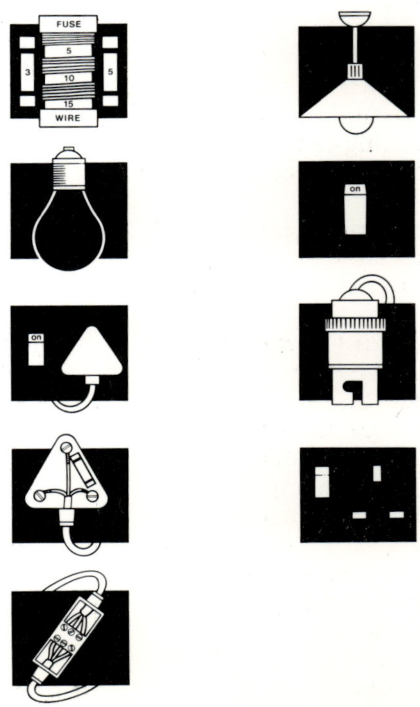

Contents

1 Introduction

There can be few homes in Britain now without a supply of electricity. It is a vital source of power that, despite the presence of other forms of fuel, is essential for those aspects of the home we take for granted – lighting, heating and the powering of many useful appliances.

It is now as important as ever that everyone has a basic knowledge of the principles of electricity and how it works. This elementary working knowledge will enable you to carry out the simple household tasks of, for example, repairing a fuse or wiring a plug onto a new appliance. These are the minimum requirements to enable you to keep the home functioning efficiently.

This book introduces electricity to those who are not familiar with it and explains the basic jobs so that anyone can tackle them. Later chapters look at more complex wiring jobs that should be well within the capabilities of the average DIY householder.

The book, however, is not just for beginners. It is a valuable reminder of how electrical work in the home should be treated – in case anyone used to tackling jobs involving electricity has got into bad habits. And we all do at some time or another!

In spelling out in simple, easy-to-follow terms the techniques involved, it cannot be stressed too heavily that any major installation work should always be checked by a qualified electrician before the final connection is made. The motto must always be: 'Better safe than sorry'.

The book concentrates on the electrical circuits in the home and how to install or wire up appliances and other electrical fittings correctly. It does not go into the more complex problems of appliances and their workings. The variations between products is such that any instructions given could not cover every possibility – and reference to a works manual for individual models is, in most cases, essential.

How electricity works

Electricity passes from the source of supply to electrical fittings or appliances along a wire – usually copper – known as a conductor. This conductor is 'live' and has either a red or brown insulation cover over it. The colour depends on whether it is a cable or a flex (see pages 42–46).

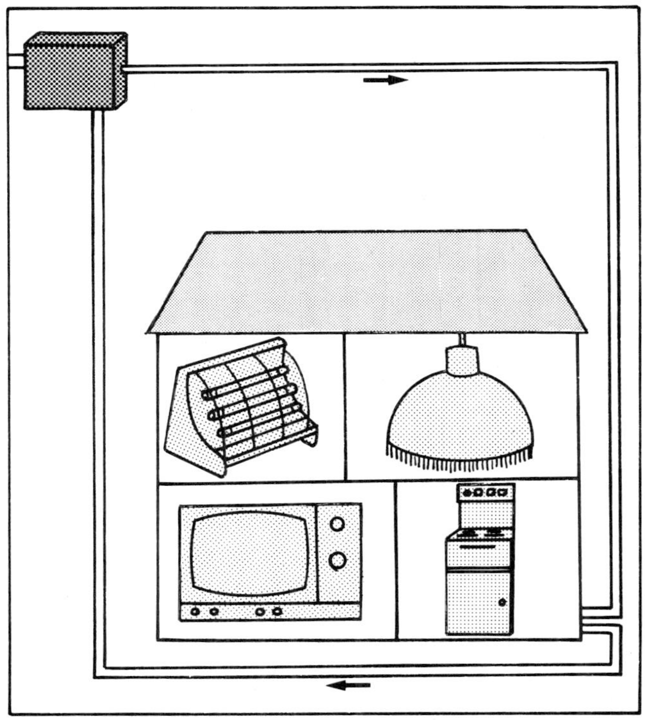

Electricity is fed into the home from a power station and via a sub-station. From the source of supply inside, it is carried along a live conductor to the various electrical fittings and appliances and returns via a neutral conductor, thus completing the circuit.

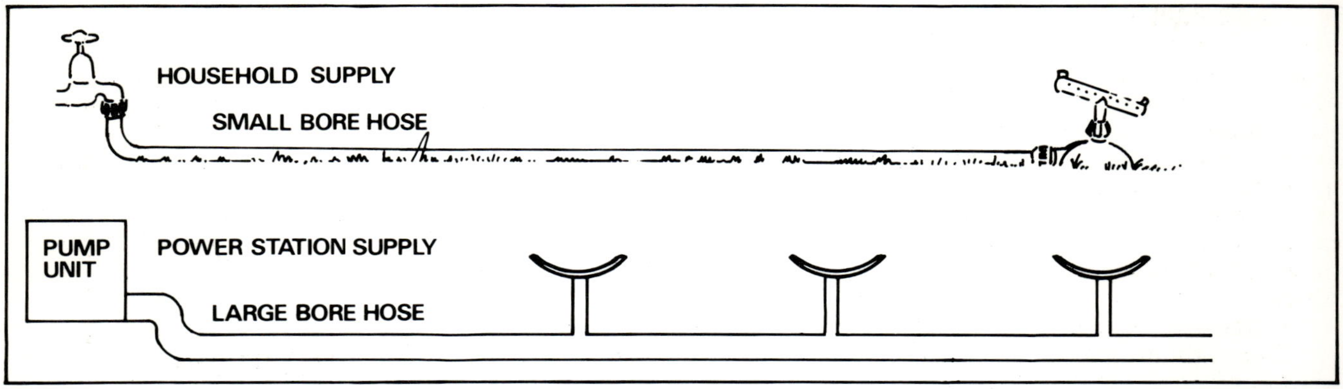

For appliances that need more electricity but, at the same time, constant pressure, the size of the conductor through which the electricity passes must be increased. One way of understanding this principle is to compare the flow of electricity with that of water. Whereas a small-bore pipe is adequate to provide water at the right pressure for a garden sprinkler, a much larger bore pipe is needed to supply water for an irrigation system, while maintaining the same pressure. If you tried to put too large a quantity of water through the smaller pipe, it would burst. So with a conductor, too much electricity and the copper wire would melt.

Having fed and operated the fitting or appliance, the electricity then passes back to the source of supply along another copper conductor, which is 'neutral'. This conductor is covered with either black or blue insulation (see pages 44–46). It is only used as the circuit is completed (that is when a fitting or appliance is switched on and in use), when the electricity passes along both conductors. If the circuit is broken, when for example a fitting or appliance is switched off – or a fault develops in the circuit – the electricity cannot pass along the conductors and so none is used.

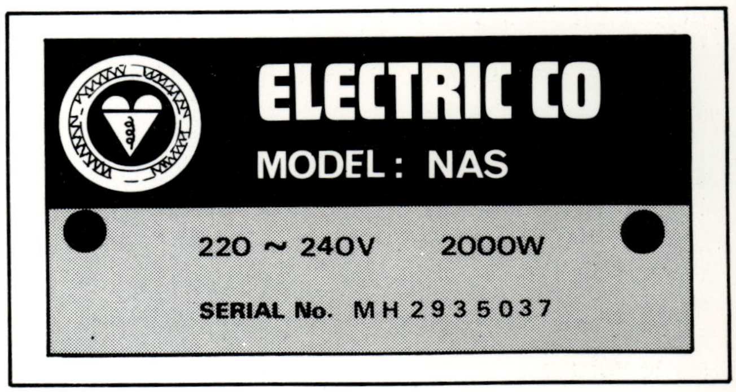

The pressure of electricity is measured in volts and in Britain this is standardised at 240 volts. The amount of electricity flowing is called the current and is measured in amperes – or amps. The power of electricity, measured in watts, is dependent on the first two. In principle, the greater the power needed for a particular appliance, the greater the current feeding it must be. On domestic appliances you will see a plate showing the voltage (normally 220–240v) and the wattage (often expressed in kilowatts – one kilowatt or kW is equivalent to 1000 watts). Always check this information.

The flow of electricity along a conductor can be compared with the flow of water along a hosepipe to a sprinkler. The pressure of the electricity is called the electromotive force and is measured in volts. The amount of electricity flowing is called the current and is measured in amperes or amps. The power of the electricity (compare the height of the water from a sprinkler) is dependent on the pressure and amount of electricity and is measured in watts. There is a formula that connects these three:

watts = volts × amps OR amps = watts ÷ volts.

Throughout Britain the pressure of electricity is standardised at 240 volts. You will see from the above formula that with a constant voltage, the higher the wattage the higher the amps required. For example:

A single 100 watt light bulb needs $\frac{100}{240} = 0.42$ amps.

A washing machine of 3000 watts needs $\frac{3000}{240} = 12.5$ amps.

As with water passing through a hosepipe you must increase the size of the pipe to allow a greater flow of water through at the same pressure, so with electricity the size of the conductor must be increased to allow a greater flow of electricity at the same voltage.

The largest permitted flow of electricity through a modern three-pin plug (see pages 47–48) is limited to 13amp. Appliances that need more electricity than this must be permanently wired in (see page 24).

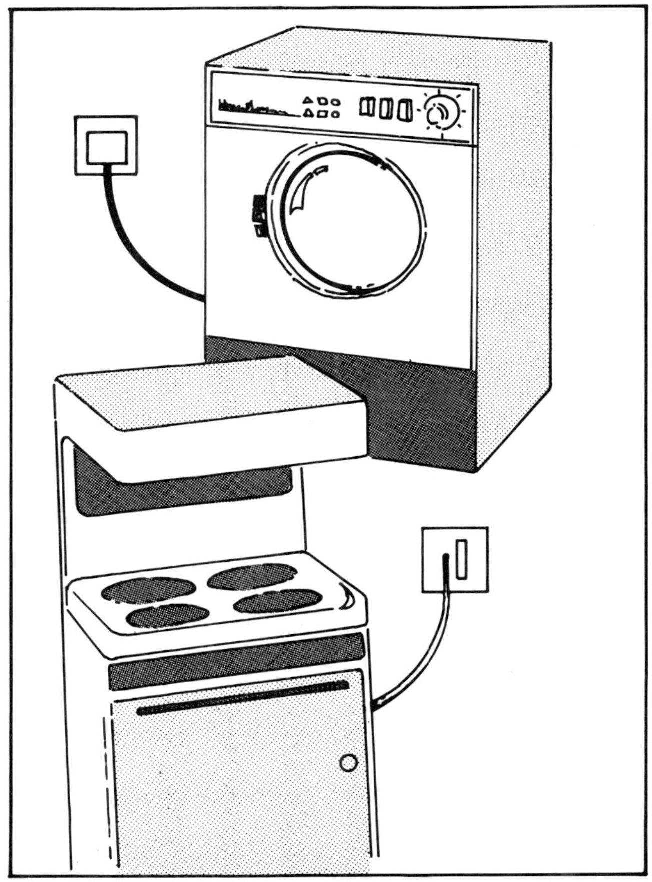

As a general rule you can plug in appliances up to 3kW provided that they are not in constant use – such as an immersion heater which is regarded as a continuous load appliance. This means that while you can plug a washing machine into a power socket outlet, an electric cooker must be wired into its own circuit direct to the consumer unit – and that circuit must carry its own fuse.

How electricity is distributed

Electricity is produced from a generator at the power station, when it is at a very high voltage. From the power station it passes into the national grid network, which distributes it to sub-stations. At these sub-stations the pressure is reduced to 240

Electricity is generated at a power station at a very high voltage. From there it travels overground via pylons (or sometimes underground) to sub-stations. Here the voltage is reduced and the electricity is then fed to a group of properties from that sub-station.

To ease the loading, there are three live outlets, so that neighbouring properties can be fed off different live conductors. There is one neutral conductor to return the electricity.

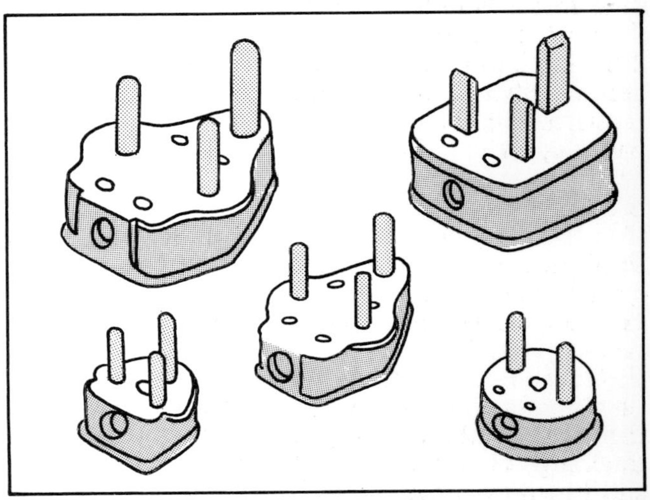

In older properties the wiring was mainly installed using lead or rubber cables. These are now obsolete and potentially dangerous where they still exist. Round-pin plugs were used to connect fittings and appliances to this system – and some of these were two-pin (live and neutral) with no earth. With the modern ring circuit, the only outlet taking a two-pin plug is that for an electric shaver, which incorporates a very low-rated fuse for safety. Modern wiring includes outlets to take 13amp rectangular-pin plugs – and each of these carries its own fuse. Unless an appliance is marked as double-insulated or is of very low wattage, such as a table lamp, it should always be wired in to earth – that is, using a three-pin plug.

volts and from here the electricity is fed into the local supply network which delivers it into your home. Inside it passes through a main fuse and a meter (which measures the amount of electricity you use) to the consumer unit.

From the consumer unit the electricity passes through various circuits to the light fittings and socket outlets. Usually the light fittings for each floor are on separate circuits – as are socket outlets. In older houses the circuits may be of the original radial type on many separate fuses (see page 74). In modern homes, or where the complete circuit has been recently rewired, the light fittings and socket outlets are usually connected to a ring main cable (see page 75).

In older houses, power socket outlets, into which appliances are connected, took round two- or three-pin plugs – in 2amp, 5amp or 15amp sizes. These are gradually becoming obsolete as old wiring is renewed. One word of warning here. Never use a high-wattage appliance – or a fitting which has metal parts – with a two-pin plug, unless the appliance is double-insulated (see pages 47–48).

With more recent systems, rectangular pins are used on plugs – except for electrical shavers, which are two-pin and require special socket outlets. Each rectangular-pin plug has its own fuse built in (see pages 33–41).

Earthing

Earthing is a very important safety feature of any electrical installation. As already described, electricity travels from the sub-station along a 'live' conductor and returns along a 'neutral' one. If a fault develops in a fitting or appliance, whereby the 'live' conductor comes into contact with the outer metal casing, this also becomes 'live'. Anyone touching this casing would then get a very nasty shock; with wet hands the result could be fatal.

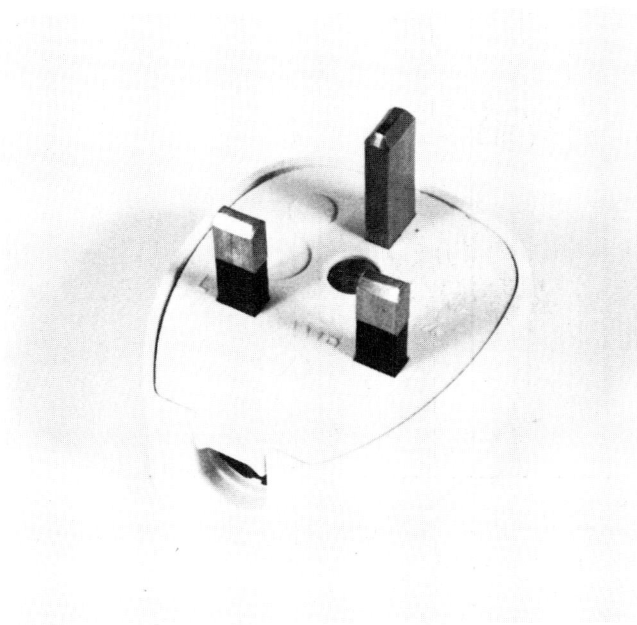

All three-pin plugs, whether with round or rectangular pins, have an earth terminal. Looking at the back of a plug, the top pin is the earth terminal, the left-hand pin the live terminal and the right-hand pin the neutral terminal.

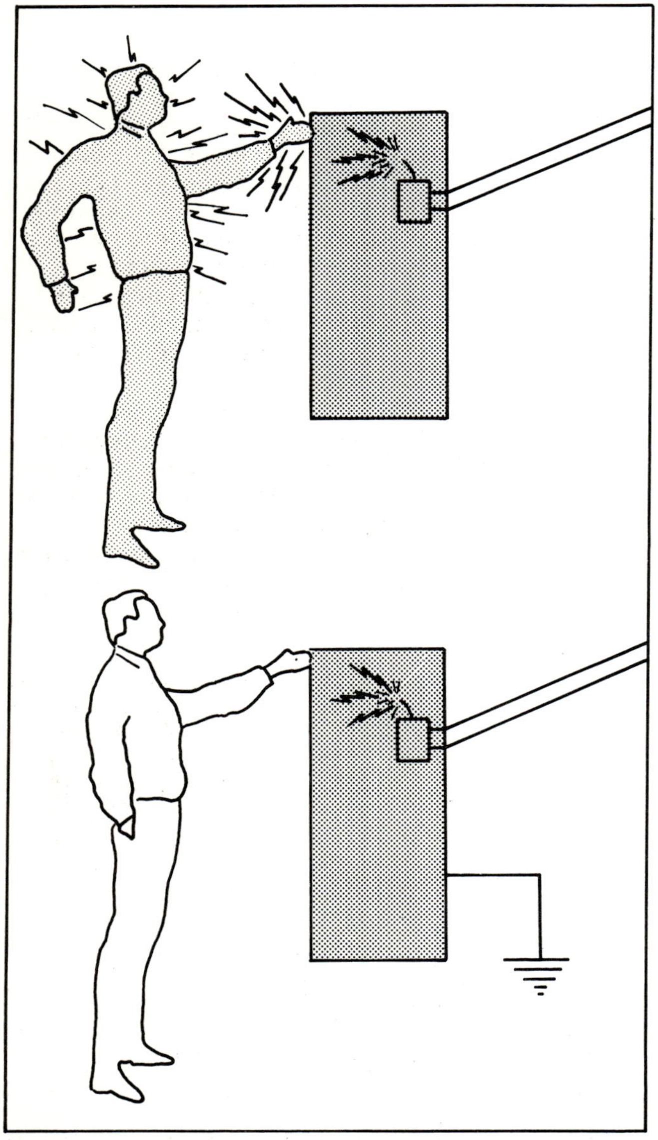

The 'neutral' pole at the sub-station is connected to earth. If there is a fault in the circuit (in this case in the appliance), the 'live' current returns to earth by any means possible. If a hand touches the 'live' casing – or any other 'live' part for that matter – the electricity will return to earth via the body.

To prevent this happening, normally the metal casing of appliances is connected electrically to earth through a conductor insulated with either a green or green and yellow cover. This 'earth' or protective conductor is connected to the earth pole in the home, which is in turn connected to the outer metal sheathing around the supply cables or, in many instances, the neutral conductor of a PME (protective multiple earth) system.

This is the reason for the third pin on plugs – both old and new. It is the 'earth' pin to which the 'earth' conductor is connected.

Earthing is needed to prevent an appliance or fitting becoming 'live', should a fault develop. In the first diagram there is a fault in the live conductor and the electricity is not returning via the neutral conductor. Instead it is running to earth through the appliance and the person touching that appliance. The person is getting an electric shock – and the result could be fatal. Although in the second diagram the same fault exists in the appliance, electricity is returning via the earth conductor, which has a lower resistance than a human's body. Therefore, although someone is touching the appliance, that person is not in danger of getting an electric shock.

2 Safety with electricity

Electricity, on which we have grown to depend so much, is a very good servant but can quite easily be a bad master. You ignore warnings and cautionary notes at your peril.

If too much current passes through a conductor, this will overheat and can easily cause the insulation protecting it to melt. The result is a short circuit and the risk of fire. Similar problems can result from worn or frayed cable or flex. Inbuilt into all circuits, therefore, is a fuse which melts when the circuit is overloaded or faulty and breaks that circuit, so the power is cut off. (For a complete explanation of fuses and how they work, see Chapter 4).

Careless fiddling or tampering with any electrical circuit can, at best, give you a nasty shock – at worst, and particularly in damp conditions, it can be fatal. Follow the basic safety rules and you will reduce the potential hazard of working with electricity.

Basic safety rules

1. Before adjusting an appliance, always switch off and remove the plug from the socket.
2. Before starting any work on a light fitting, wall switch or socket outlet, switch off at the main consumer unit; don't assume, for example, that it is sufficient just to turn off a light at the wall switch. You can take out the relevant fuse in the consumer unit, thus enabling you to use lights and power elsewhere in the home. But always check with a test meter that the circuit is not live and that no-one can turn it on until work is finished.

Working on any 'live' appliance (when it is still plugged in and switched on) is asking for trouble. As soon as you remove the cover, you will probably be exposing 'live' conductors and terminals. The chances of getting an electric shock, particularly if one hand is touching a 'live' part and the other an earthed part, are great – in which case the full mains voltage will be running through the body.

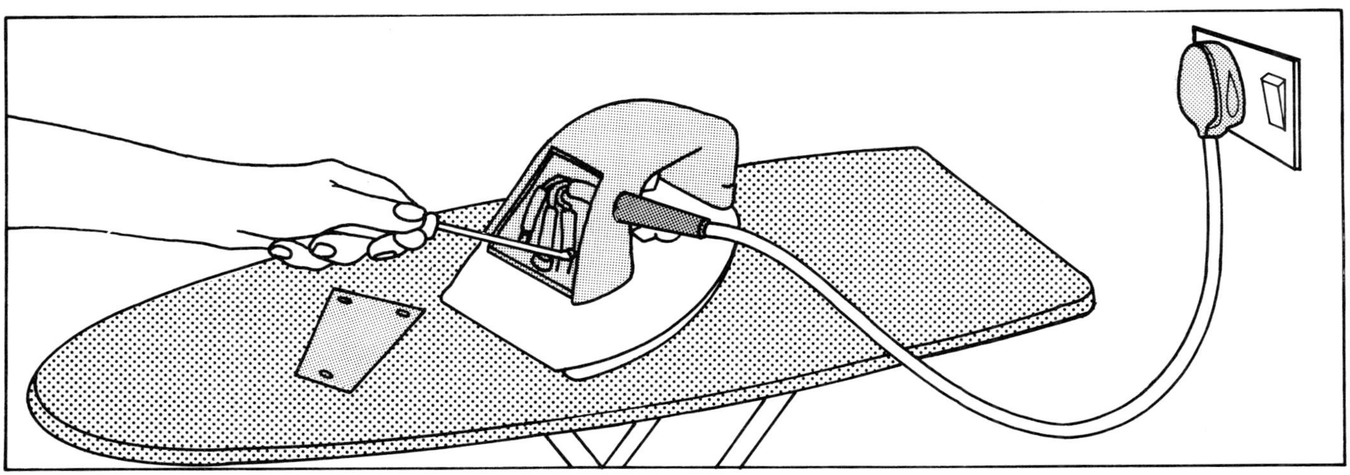

3. Never connect any appliance to a light fitting with a bayonet plug; always use a three-pin wall plug.
4. Always use a plug to connect an appliance to the main supply; never poke bare conductors into the socket outlet.
5. Always fit rubberised plugs to any appliance that is likely to undergo heavy or rough treatment – such as electric drills, garden tools, etc.
6. Always unplug appliances when not in use.
7. Always unplug appliances before filling them with water – for example kettles, steam irons and hair curlers – or with other liquids.

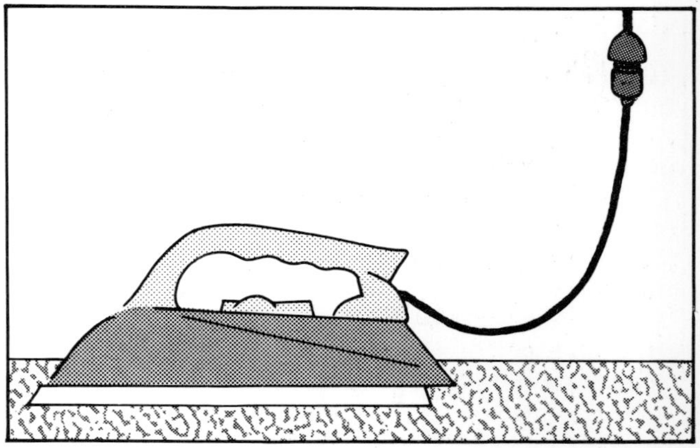

There is a double danger in plugging an appliance into a light socket. Not only is there no earth connection in the event of a fault, but you could also be overloading the light circuit and the lamp flex. This could lead to overheating and an eventual breakdown of the insulation and the lampholder.

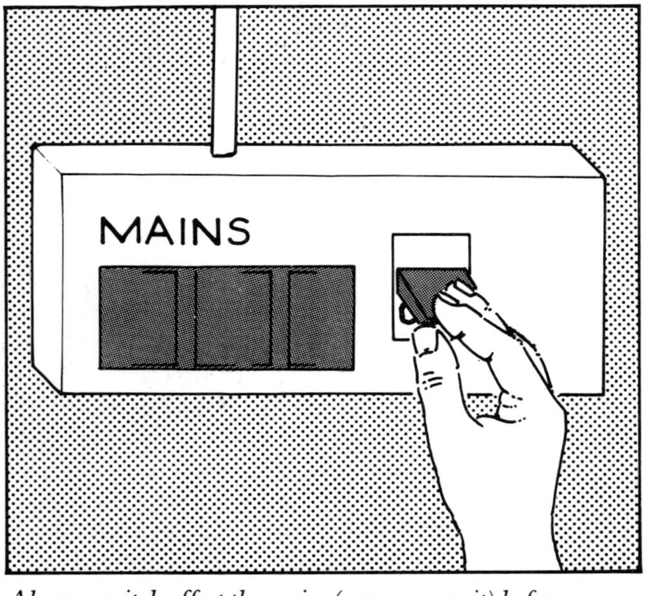

Always switch off at the mains (consumer unit) before working on any electrical fitting. It is not sufficient to switch off at the fitting, since this only isolates the live conductor outlet. The connections within the fitting may still be 'live'.

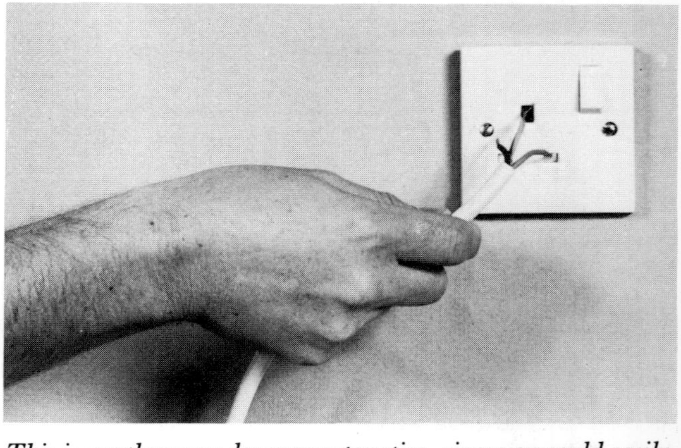

This is another very dangerous practice, since you could easily get a shock when inserting the conductors. The connections will invariably be weaker than when using the conventional method and a poor earth connection will result in an unearthed appliance.

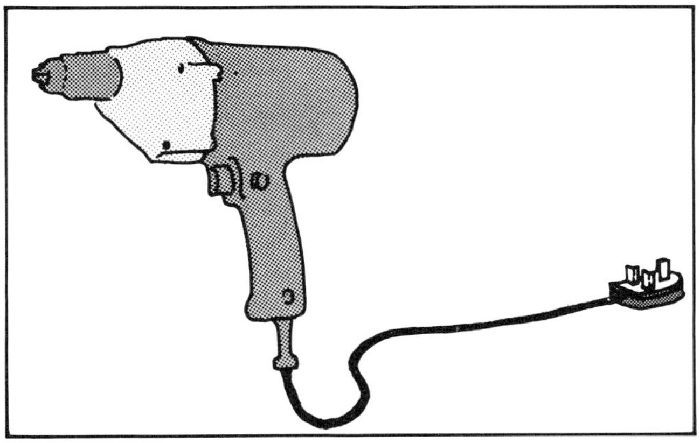

Hard plastic plugs shatter easily, so with those appliances that are liable to be subjected to rough treatment always fit a rubber plug. Then you will have no fear of damaging the plug and making it unsafe.

Never fill an appliance with fluid while it is still plugged in. If any fluid is spilt over the side of the appliance, it could run down and get onto the connectors or socket – and the combination of water and electricity could be fatal.

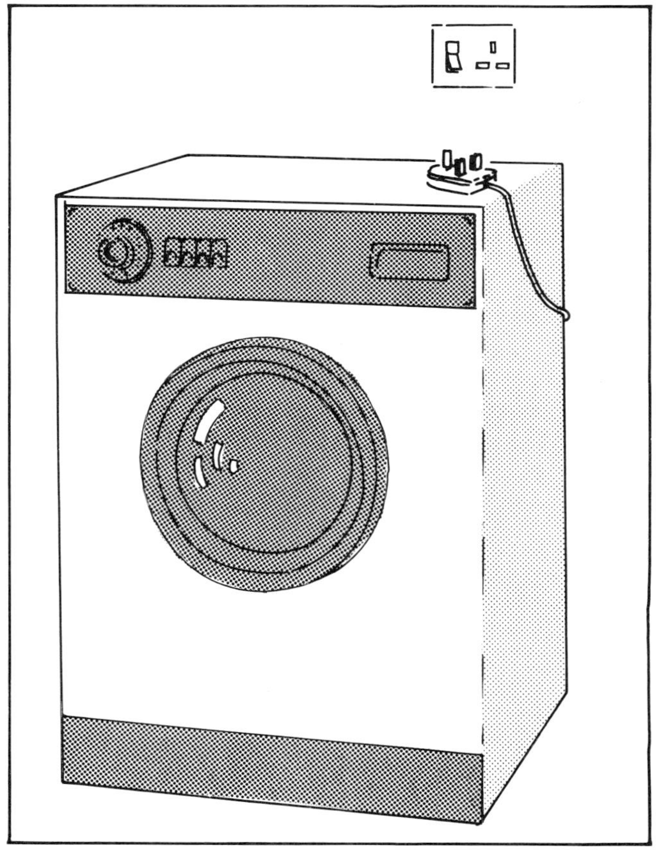

Always unplug an appliance that is not in use and place the plug and flex in a safe position. For one reason, there is then no chance of that appliance being accidentally switched on – by a young child, for example, fiddling with the controls.

8. Never join sections of flex by twisting the conductor wires together and binding them with insulating tape. If you must join lengths of flex, use a flex connector; better still, replace the length of flex with a longer piece.
9. Avoid long trailing flexes over which people may accidentally trip.
10. Never run a flex under floor coverings; the wear will soon damage it.
11. Don't stretch flex to its limit, for example when using a vacuum cleaner; you will only weaken the connections.

Trailing flexes are exposed to much greater wear and tear than would otherwise be the case – and the flex is not designed to be walked over! And there is the obvious danger of someone tripping over the flex, which could damage both the appliance or fitting and the connections.

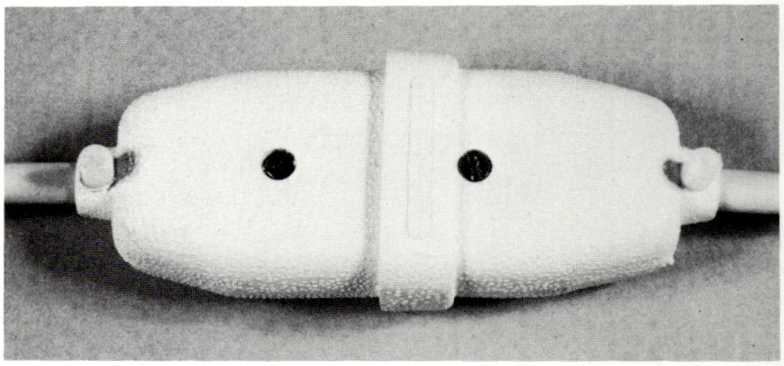

Always use connectors to join flex. If you simply twist conductors together and tape them, there is a danger that they will pull apart if subjected to strain, and could be damaged if accidentally trodden on. Equally important is the fact that with this type of join the electricity will not be conducted so easily – and this could lead to overheating, a breakdown of the insulation and worse.

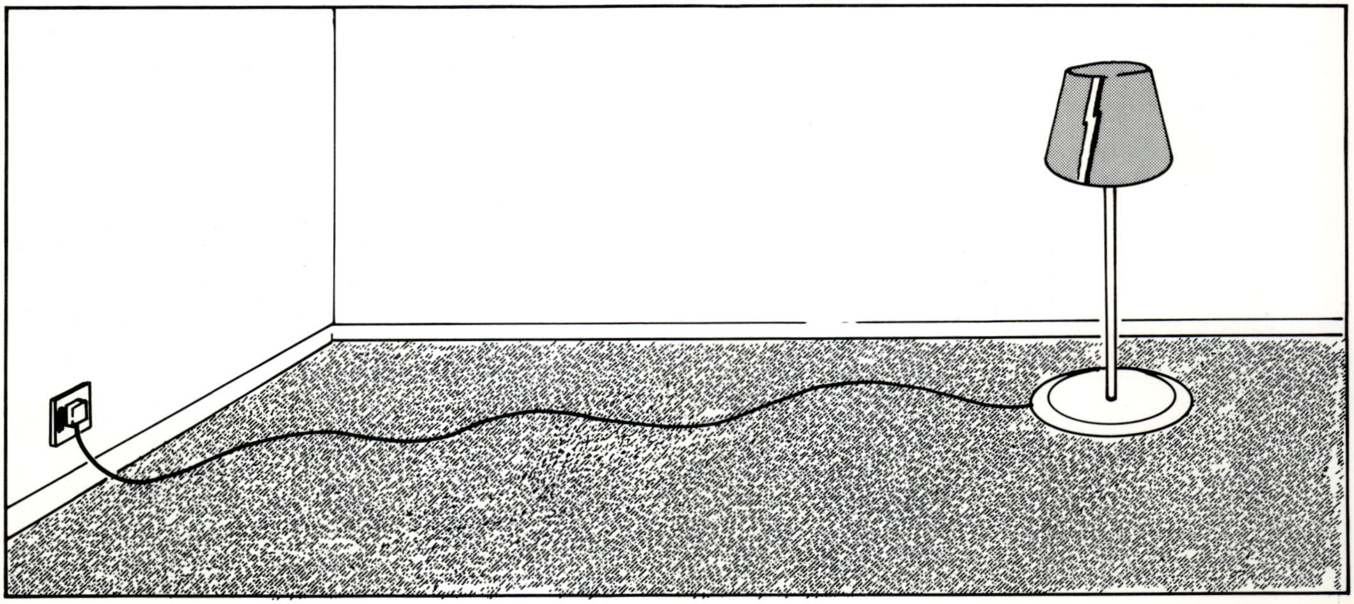

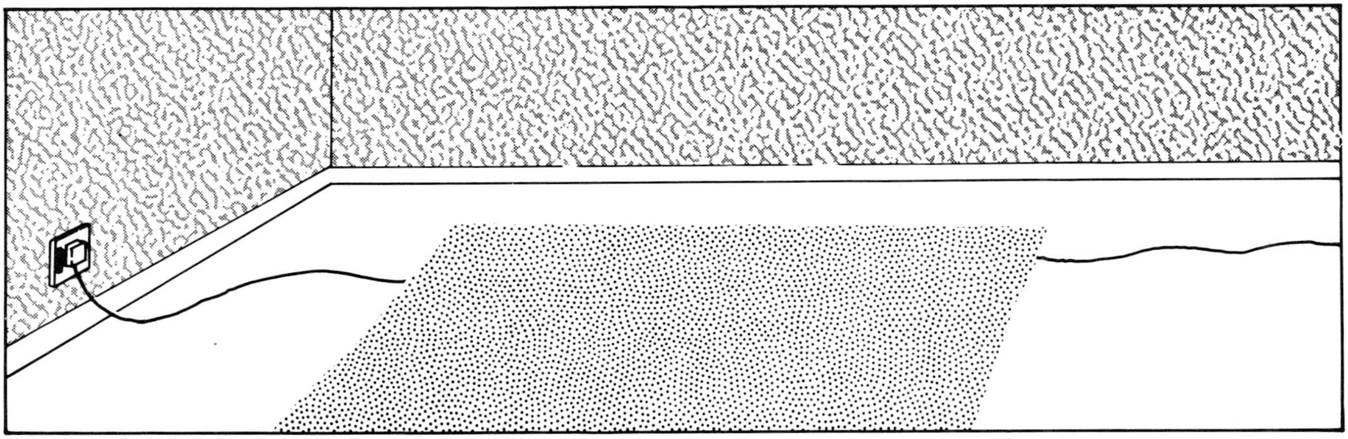

Wear and tear is again the hazard if you allow flex to run under carpets and rugs. The flex will be trodden on, and may be twisted, stretched or torn – and the added danger here is that as you cannot see the flex damage may not be detected until it is too late.

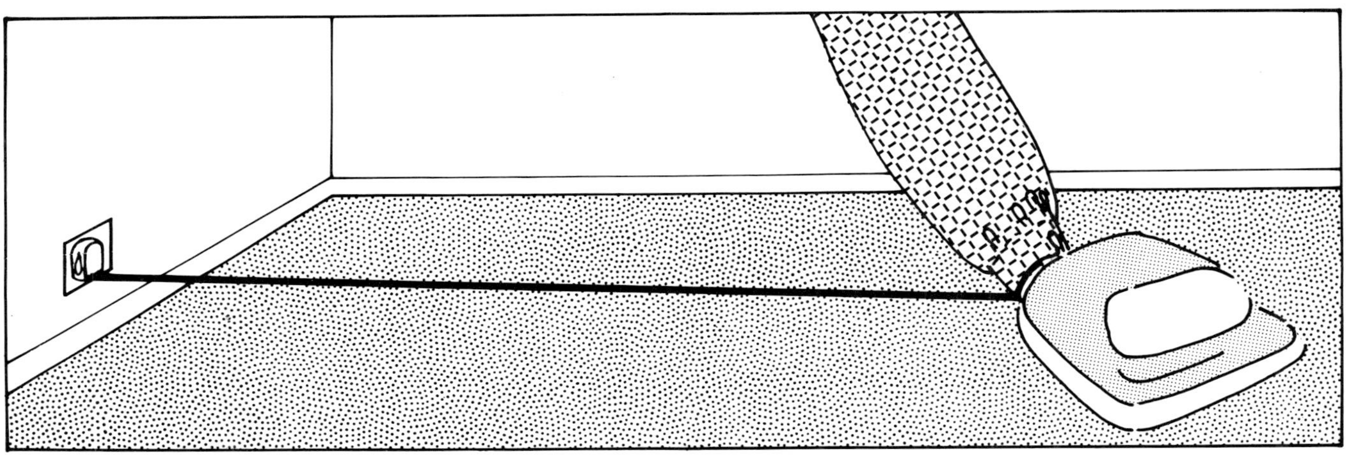

Overstretching the flex on such appliances as vacuum cleaners will weaken the connections at either end, leading to over-heating and a potential fire risk. Always make sure you are using a convenient socket and take care that the flex does not become trapped around a chair or table leg, for example.

12. Never pull a plug from its socket by means of the flex; again this will weaken the connections.
13. Don't try to 'patch up' a damaged or worn piece of flex with insulating tape; the only safe method of repair is to replace it.
14. Use orange-coloured flex for all outdoor jobs, since it shows up much better against the background.
15. Always unroll extension cable when using it; if you leave it rolled up, it could eventually overheat.
16. Make sure you have adequate lighting in potential danger areas, such as in halls and the kitchen and on stairs and landings.

You should never remove a plug from the socket outlet by pulling at the flex. Again you will risk the hazards of weakened connections.

When using appliances outside – and in particular gardening equipment – make sure you have an orange flex fitted, since this shows up much better against grass or a hedge background and reduces the chances of accidentally running over or cutting through the flex.

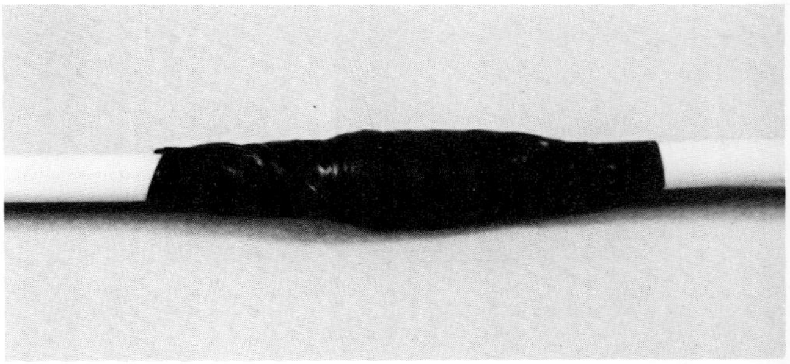

Despite the convenience of patching up worn or damaged flex with insulating tape, this is a dangerous practice since there is a strong possibility of conductors touching and causing a short circuit – leading to a fire risk. Always replace worn or damaged flex.

Even though you may not need the full length of an extension lead, never use it rolled up for long periods. With current passing through the whole length, the coiled flex will soon overheat and this could damage the insulation, melt the conductors and lead to a short circuit – and possibly fire.

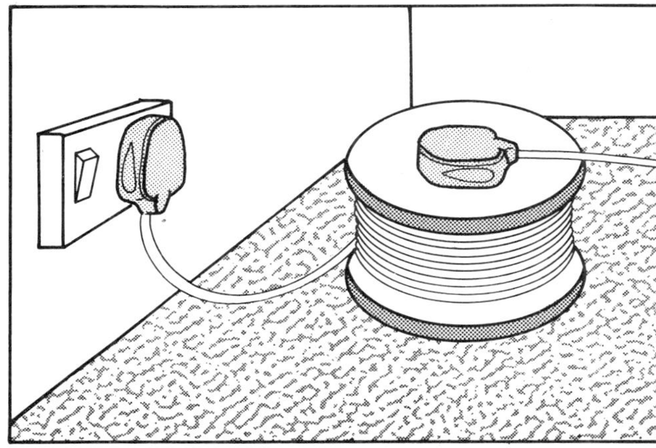

The kitchen is one of the major areas in the home where potential dangers lurk unseen. The combination of high-powered appliances and the continual presence of liquids makes it essential to have an area that is well-lit, so that you can work efficiently and safely.

17. Never touch a switch when your hands are wet; the only exception is a cord-pull switch, for example in the bathroom.
18. Never use a two- or three-way adaptor for high-powered appliances; because of the amount of electricity these need, they must never share a single socket outlet.

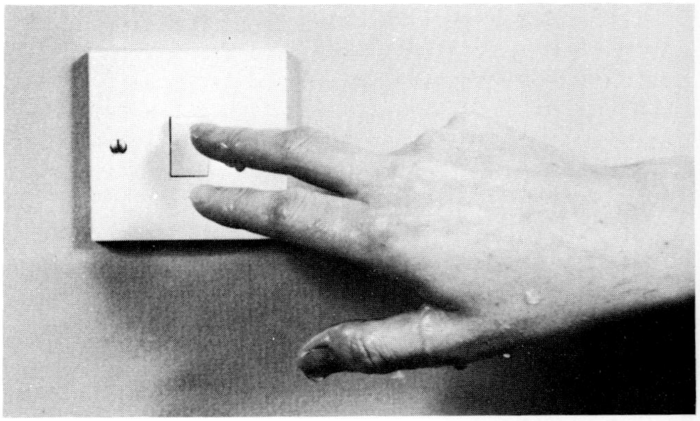

Keep wet hands well away from switches – and any electrical fitting or appliance, for that matter. Water can easily seep through the mechanism and onto the terminals or conductors with serious results.

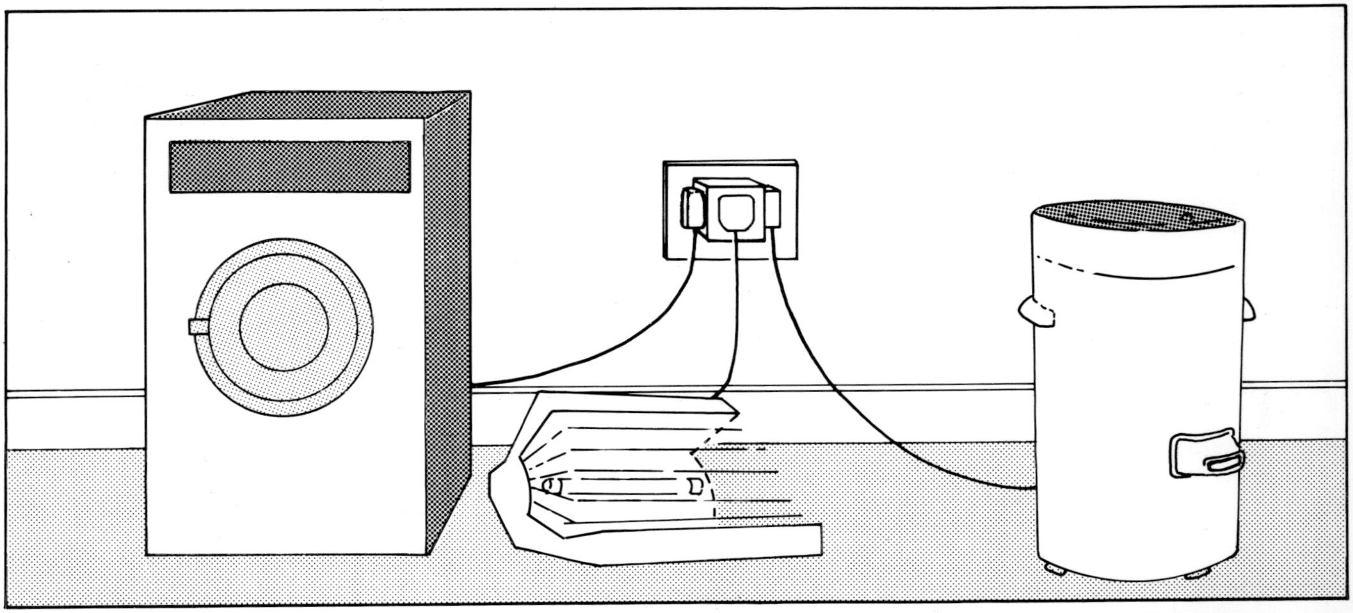

You must never run two high-powered appliances off a single socket outlet with the help of an adaptor. With the example here, the total loading is 5kW – and if the adaptor is unfused, that and the socket outlet could overheat. Equally, you must never use two adaptors on one socket outlet.

The need for earthing

Electricity, as already discussed in Chapter 1, is fed in and out of the home by two conductors. One is the 'live' conductor, which brings the power in; the other is the 'neutral' conductor, which returns the current to the sub-station (see pages 7–8).

If a fault develops in an appliance in which the metal casing of the appliance is in contact with the live wire, the casing will also be live and therefore dangerous, since you could get a very nasty shock – or worse – if you accidentally touch it. This is why appliances are either double-insulated or fitted with a three-core flex. The third, green and yellow conductor must always be connected to earth (see pages 11–12). By earthing the casing, the current can return to the earthed neutral pole at the sub-station. The risk of getting a shock is therefore eliminated.

All appliances or lamps with a metal casing or any metal parts which are exposed and therefore likely to be touched by hand must have a three-core flex, which includes, with the live and neutral conductors, an earth conductor, enabling you to earth the appliance or light fitting and make it 'safe'. The only exceptions to this are appliances that are 'double-insulated'. These appliances incorporate a fail-safe design with no 'live' external parts and carry a double-insulation symbol. These appliances are fitted with two-core flex.

Safety in the bathroom

With the presence of water – with the possibility of splashing, certainly wet bare skin and often a damp atmosphere – the bathroom is potentially the most dangerous room in the home. For this reason, special safety rules apply.

In general, all appliances should be fitted with three-core flex, with the earth (green/yellow) connected to the earth terminal in the plug. Some appliances, however, are double-insulated and are therefore fitted with a two-core flex (live and neutral). These are quite safe, as long as they carry the correct symbol (a double square).

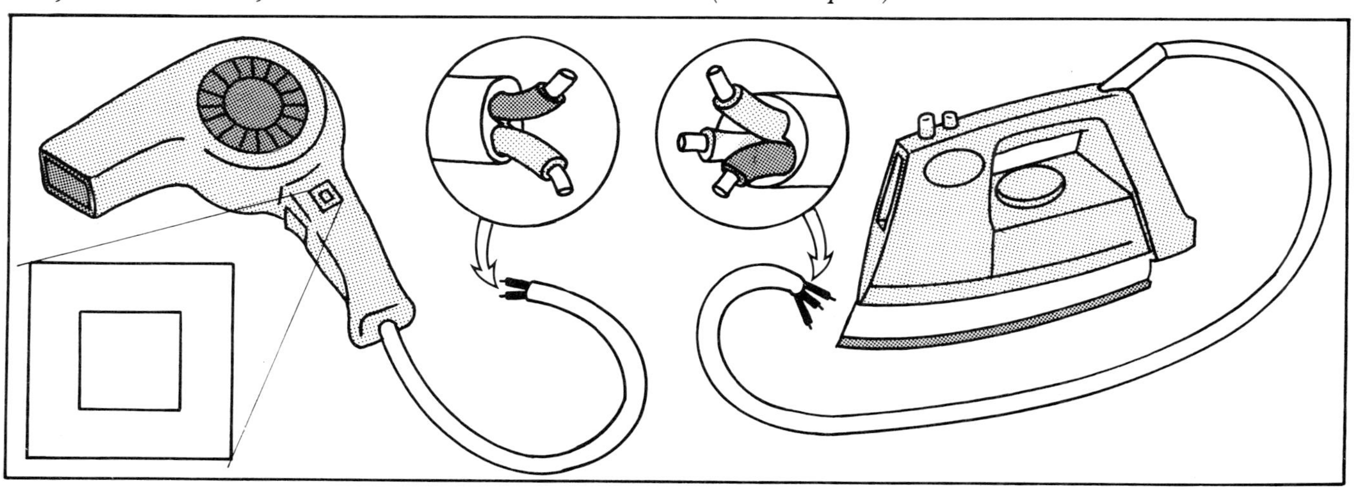

1. All switched fittings must be operated only by cord-pull type switches, for example, lights and wall or overhead heaters.
2. No socket outlets are allowed in this room, apart from shaver sockets which have an isolating transformer with a micro-amp fuse.
3. Striplights must be of a special type that ensures the power supply is automatically cut off from both ends of the light holder when the tube is removed.

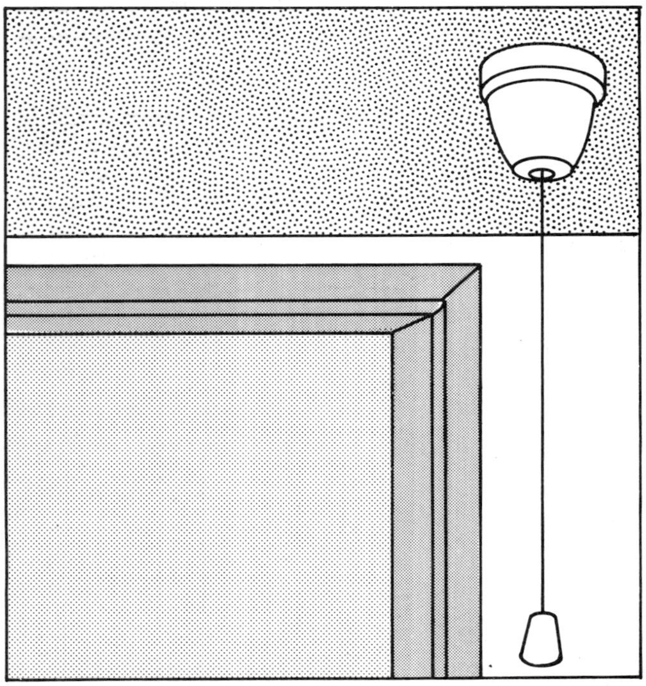

To avoid the danger of touching a standard switch with wet hands, in the bathroom any switched appliance must be operated with a cord-pull switch. The electrical connections should be high up on the wall or ceiling, well out of reach.

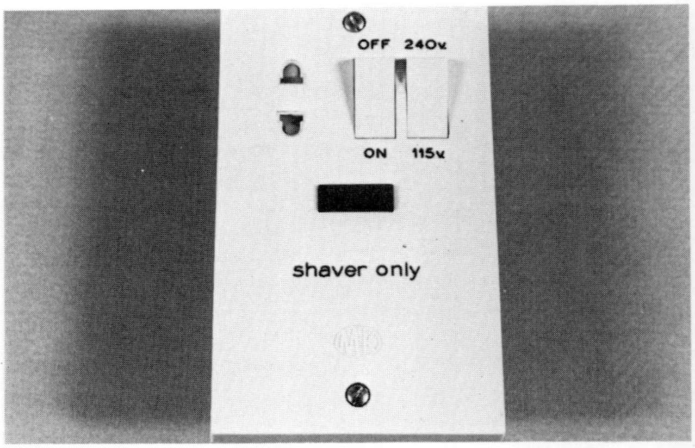

The only exposed socket outlet permitted in a bathroom is that for an electric shaver. Not only is the shaver double-insulated, but the socket itself carries a very low-rated fuse, which will blow if anything other than a shaver is plugged into it.

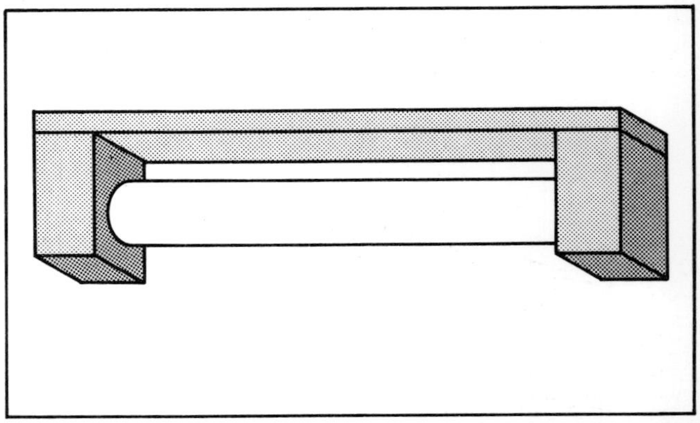

The safety striplight is essential for use in the bathroom. It is designed in such a way that you cannot remove the tube without automatically isolating the connections at either end, thus eliminating any danger from wet hands on live connectors.

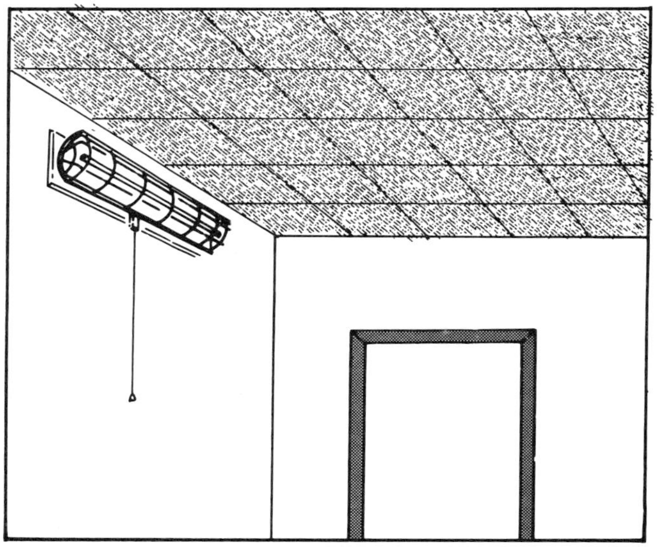

4. Any bar or tube electric heating must be located high up and out of normal reach – on a wall or the ceiling.
5. No mains-operated portable appliances should be brought into the bathroom, even by means of an extension lead from another room.

The reason for having a bathroom heater high on the wall – or fitted to the ceiling – is obvious. Here it is well out of reach of wet hands or splashing water.

The presence of water and moisture in the bathroom could prove fatal if it gets into an electrical appliance or any part of its wiring. Therefore you must never bring a mains-operated appliance into the bathroom, even by means of an extension lead.

Safety in the kitchen

The kitchen will normally contain the most appliances – and those consuming the most power. Again the presence of water and the inevitable condensation – even if you have extractor fans – means similar hazards to those in the bathroom can exist.

Electrical appliances must be treated with the same respect as anywhere else in the home. As a general rule, the kitchen should have plenty of socket outlets, but these should be safely and conveniently placed – and well away from the sink or other washing areas.

High-load appliances (over 13amp) must always be wired in to their own circuit and carry their own fuse. Never try to plug them in to the normal power circuit.

1. Electric cookers are very high current users and must be permanently wired into a special power switch.
2. The washing machine should have its own power point. When the heating element is operating, the power demand from the machine is such that the maximum current a normal 13amp plug can handle is flowing. If the machine is plugged into an adaptor and a second appliance is also in use off that adaptor the circuit will overload, the socket may be damaged and there is a possible risk of fire.

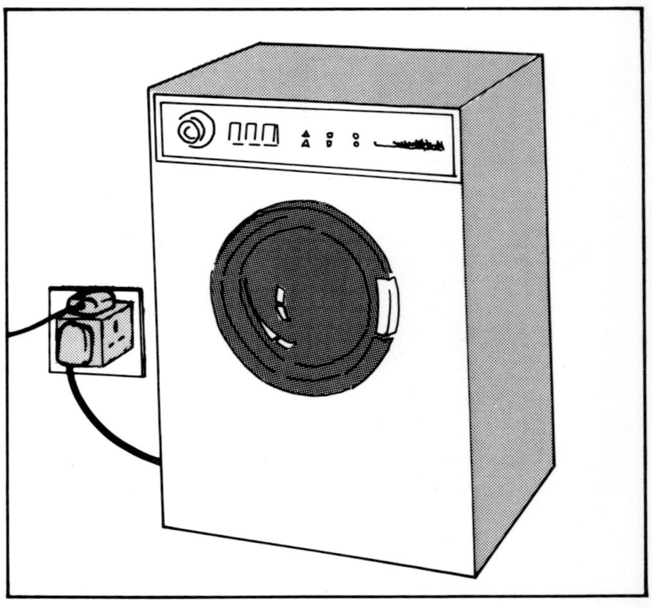

Since a washing machine takes the maximum load permissible on an 13amp circuit, there is no spare load for another appliance. Therefore you should never use it plugged in to an adaptor in case a second appliance is used from that adaptor while the washing machine is in operation.

3. Always unplug an appliance before washing it or wiping it down with a damp cloth.
4. Always dry your hands before touching a switch or plug.
5. Never hold a full saucepan or other container over an appliance where it could spill.
6. Make sure your lighting system gives you sufficient light wherever you need it to enable you to see clearly what you are doing.
7. Never have flexes trailing anywhere near or over hotplates or anything with a sharp edge that could cut through the insulation. In general, avoid long flexes.

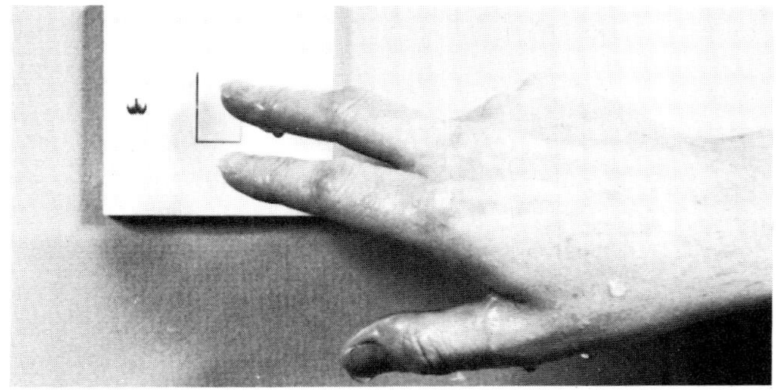

The chances are that you will be working in the kitchen with wet hands. Never be tempted to operate a switch until you have dried them – even just to turn off the kettle.

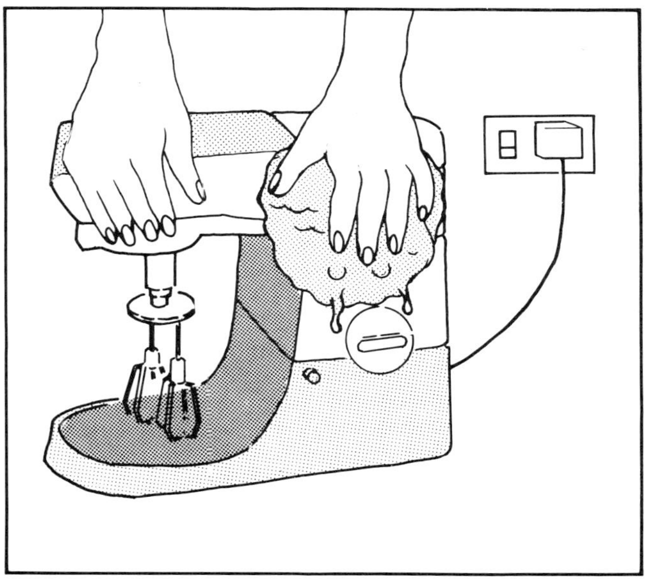

Never try to wash or clean an appliance while it is still plugged in. Even with a damp cloth, water may penetrate into the mechanism and the results could be very dangerous. Water and electricity don't mix!

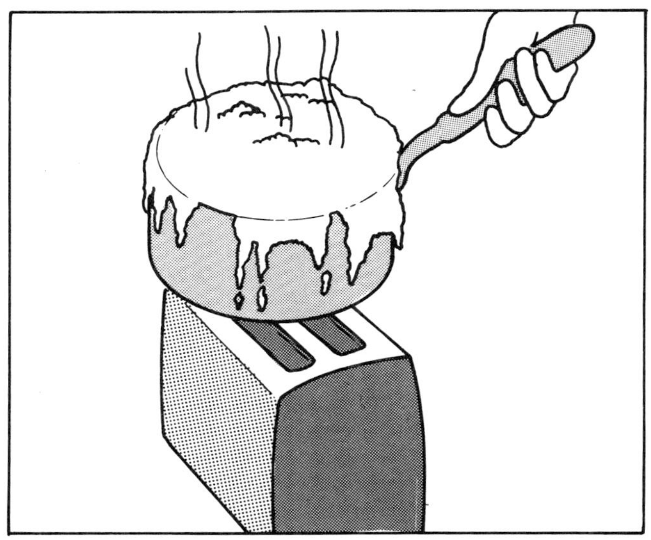

When carrying liquids about the kitchen, keep them well away from electrical appliances. If any is spilt into an appliance that is switched on, you are likely to cause a short circuit and blow the fuse.

Good lighting in a kitchen – particularly above work surfaces – will help you work efficiently and reduce the chances of accidents.

Trailing flexes are potentially more dangerous in the kitchen than anywhere else. One example is having flex trailing over a cooker, which you might accidentally switch on without first removing the flex. And there are always sharp instruments, such as knives, lying about which could easily damage flex.

3 Tools and Equipment

The basic tools listed here are essential for the day-to-day maintenance of your electrical system. It is always a wise precaution to keep a card of fuse wire or packet of cartridge fuses, a screwdriver and a torch over the main consumer unit. This will save those moments of panic and hunting round in the dark if a fuse should blow at night – when, of course, it normally does!

Pliers A pair of 150mm (6in) pliers, preferably with plastic-covered handles, is a must for twisting heavy conductors together, cutting wires and general gripping operations. Make sure the pliers have wire-cutting facilities.

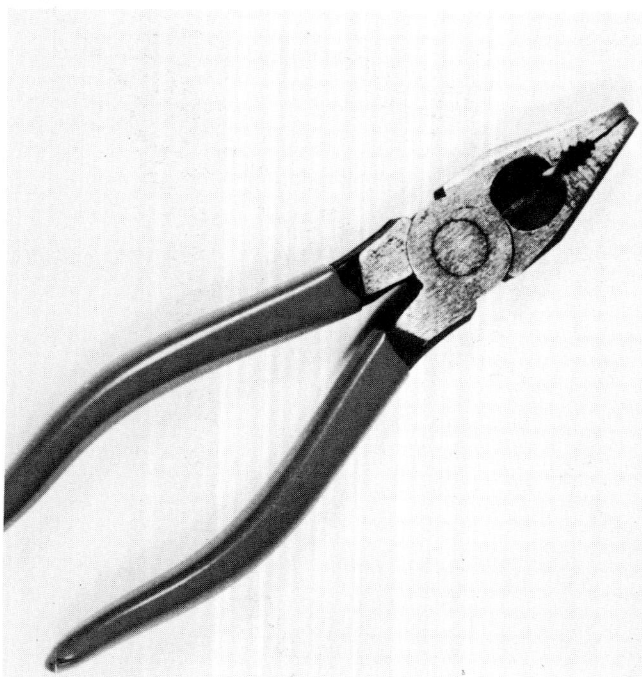

Screwdrivers Ideally you should have two: a small insulated screwdriver, with a blade of about 3mm (1/8in) and incorporating a neon tester, and a bigger one about 150mm (6in) long with a 5mm (3/16in) blade preferably with an insulated sleeve over the shank to reduce the chances of getting a shock, should the screw you are working on be live. The neon tester screwdriver will indicate whether there is current going into the screw since it has a tiny bulb at the end which lights up.

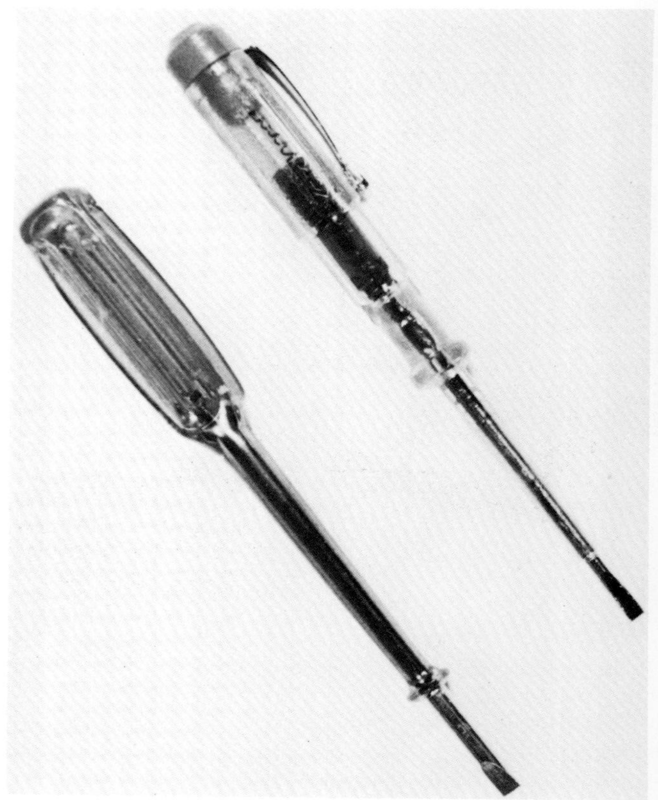

Torch Most of the electrical wiring and connections in the home are tucked away out of sight – in a cupboard, under the floorboards or in the loft. Therefore a powerful lantern torch is invaluable to give you plenty of light in which to work.

Wire strippers Although you can strip the insulation of the conductors of flex or cable with a suitable pair of pliers, wire strippers are much easier to use and with them there is much less chance of damaging the cores. Various types are available and most incorporate a cutter and basic screwdriver.

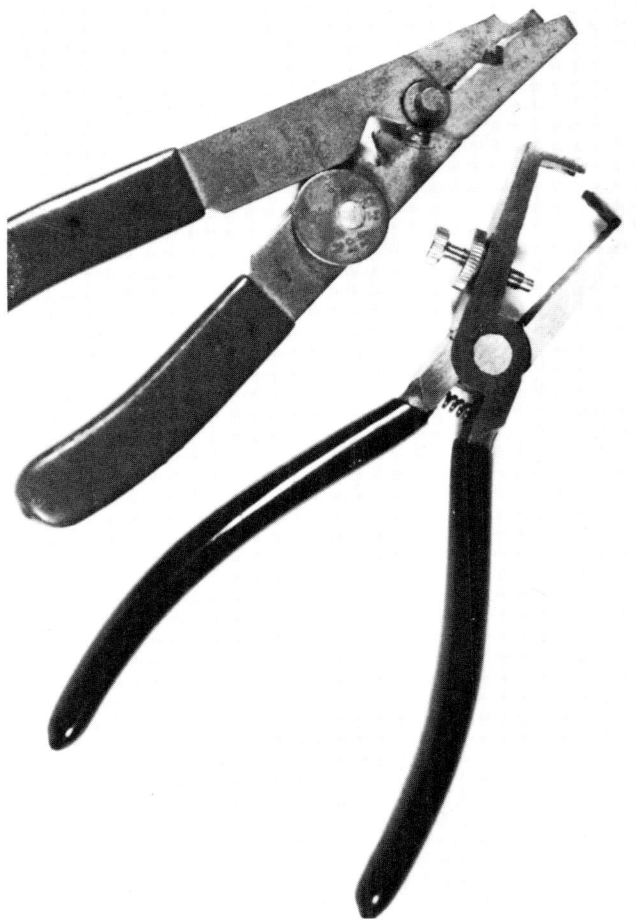

Cutting knife You will need a sharp cutting knife to strip the outer insulation from flexes and cables, particularly the heavier PVC-coated types. Use one with interchangeable blades so you can replace a blunt blade quickly and easily. But work carefully to avoid cutting right through the flex or cable; if you do, you will have to start again – and will have a shorter length as a result.

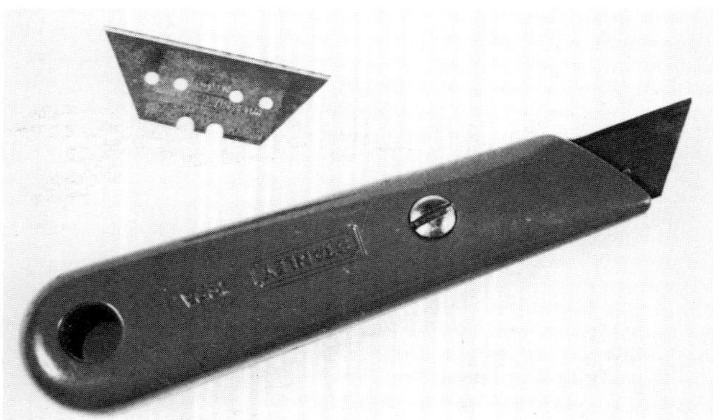

Insulating tape Uses of insulating tape include binding cut sections of flex that is textile-braided to prevent the outer insulation from unthreading. But tape should not be used to join lengths of flex or cable.

Fuses (wire or cartridge) Depending on the type of fuses installed in your electrical circuit, keep a supply of either fuse wire or cartridges handy in case a fuse blows. The 13amp plugs take 3amp and 13amp fuses (to BS 1362) and consumer units take 5amp, 15amp, 30amp and 45amp fuses (to BS 1361).

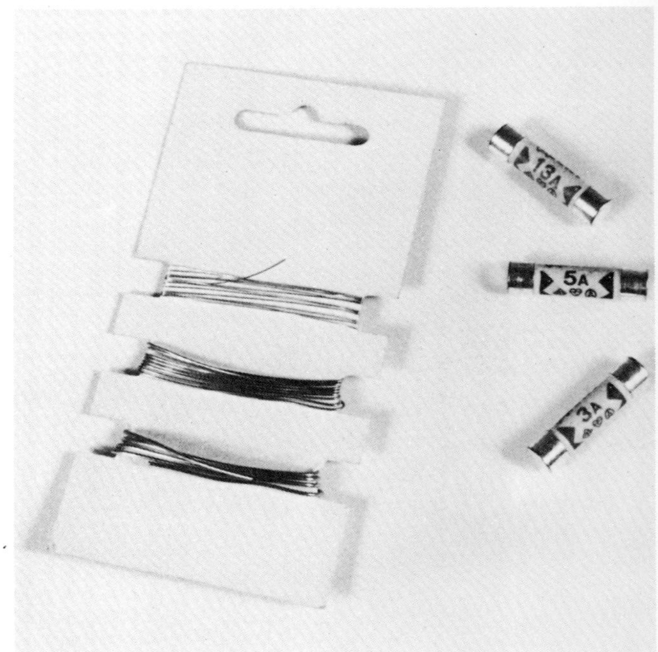

While the above tools and equipment are essential for general maintenance and repair work on the circuit, there are other items that you will need if you want to open up and repair appliances. These will depend on individual requirements and therefore a comprehensive list would not be practical. But the following items will almost certainly be needed for any additional electrical work.

Pozidriv or Supadriv screwdrivers Numbers 1 and 2 will fit the screws used in most appliances. Make sure when buying these screwdrivers that you are not getting the now-obsolete Phillips cross-head type, since this is not suitable for Pozidriv screws. As a guide, Pozidriv and Supadriv screwdrivers will never be chromium-plated.

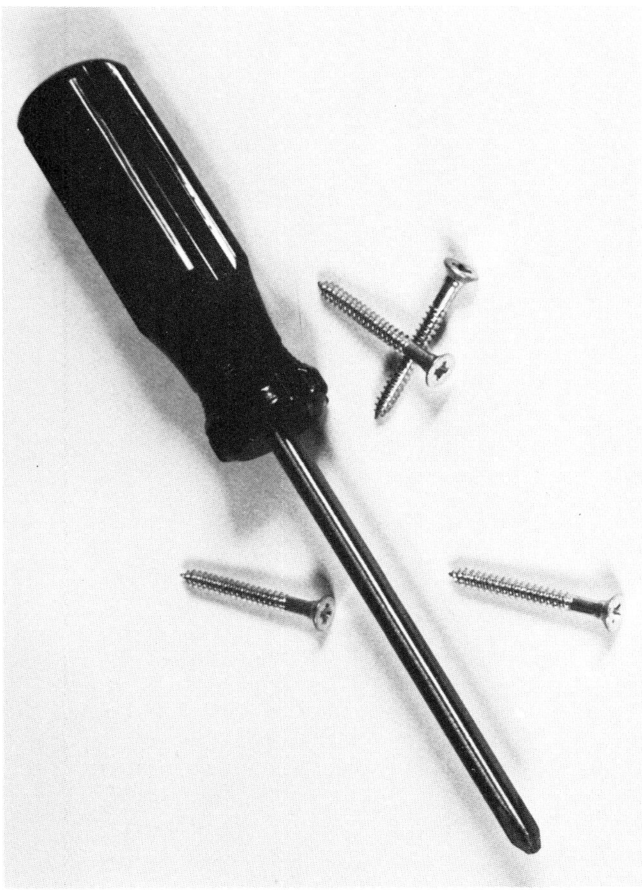

Set of small spanners It is bad practice to use pliers or other similar tools on hexagon nuts as you will probably damage the nuts and then you may not be able to loosen them. Most modern appliances use metric nuts, but you will find BA sizes on some older appliances. Both metric and BA sets of small spanners are available.

Large screwdriver An insulated 8mm (3⁄8in) blade screwdriver is a useful addition for any larger screws you may come across. Remember the screwdriver blade should always fit the screw slot; if you use a smaller screwdriver, you will eventually damage the slot and won't be able to remove the screw.

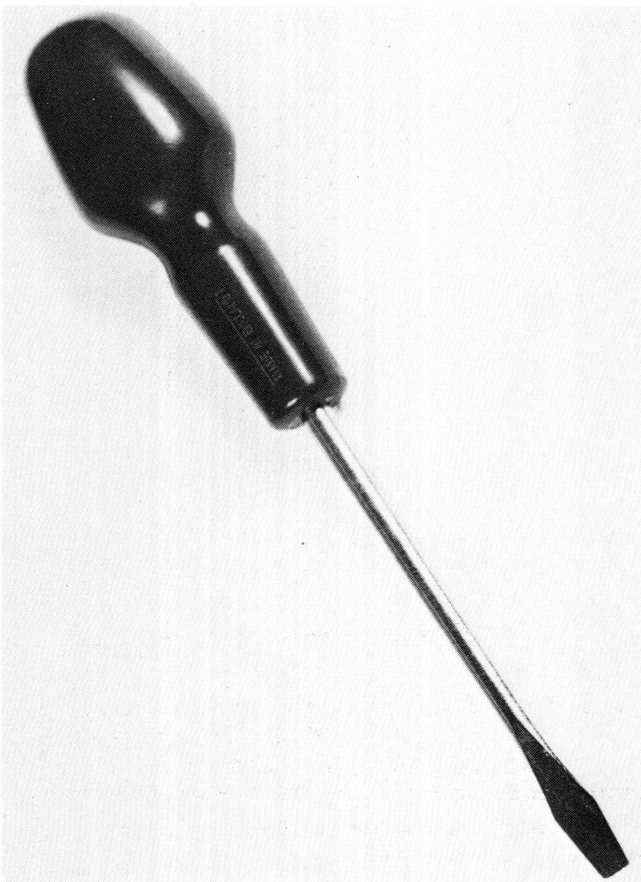

Soldering iron and soft solder You can get electric or the cheaper gas-heated soldering irons; you will also need solder and flux. You will find certain electrical connections are soldered – in, for example, radios. If you break the original connections, possibly to change a damaged wire, you will have to solder the new wire back in place.

4 Fuses

When an electrical current passes through a conductor, it generates heat. For the same amount of current, a thin conductor will heat up more – and quicker – than a thick one. If too much current is passed through a domestic cable it will heat up to such an extent that a fire may result.

Fuses are fitted into each circuit to prevent this happening. A fuse is a short piece of thin wire that will heat up and melt when current above a specified rating passes through it. This causes the circuit to be broken – and stops the overloading.

In the normal home system, there are three main types of fuse: a mains fuse, a consumer unit fuse and a plug fuse.

Mains fuse This is fitted between the mains supply and the meter. It is a highly-rated fuse which very rarely blows. It is sealed by the Electricity Board and can only be replaced by them.

As electricity enters your home, it is fed through the mains fuse box. This is the property of the Electricity Board and should never be tampered with by the consumer. Normally faults on the circuit cause a fuse within the circuit to blow. But, in extreme situations, the main fuse will blow to protect other consumers fed from the same sub-station. From the main fuse box electricity runs through the meter, which measures the amount you are using, to the consumer unit, which contains the fuses for each circuit in the home and from where the wiring in the home is the responsibility of the consumer. The switch on the consumer unit isolates the supply from the mains and enables you to work safely on the various circuits as required.

Consumer unit fuses These are fitted into the main consumer unit and may be replaced by the householder. There are three variations:

Inside the consumer unit you will find a set of fuses, each one controlling a separate circuit. For lighting circuits – up to 1kW – the fuse is rated at 5amp. The ring main circuits are fused at 30amp and can carry a loading up to 7.2kW. Intermediate fuses are available for such things as immersion heaters and storage heaters. The highest rated fuse is usually 45amp, which will control a cooker circuit and offers a loading of up to 10.8kW. On one side of the consumer unit is a switch, which will control the supply to the unit – and hence on through the circuits. Three different types of fuse can be used in a consumer unit – rewirable, cartridge and miniature circuit breakers, not so much fuses as special switches that turn themselves off if a circuit is overloaded or faulty. When the problem is solved you switch them back on.

a) Rewirable fuses These are the traditional fuses and comprise a short piece of fuse wire stretched between two screws. When the fuse blows, a new piece of wire of the correct rating is fitted in its place.
b) Cartridge fuses With these, the fuse is contained in a replaceable cartridge. Various ratings are available. The cartridges are of different sizes and with different colour flashes to prevent you replacing the wrong one.
c) Miniature circuit breakers (mcb) These are not really fuses, but rather special switches that automatically turn off if too much current tries to pass through. They are more expensive than fuses, but require no replacement – and are becoming increasingly popular. When the mcb is tripped off by too much current, all you need to do is to rectify the fault and then re-set the switch.

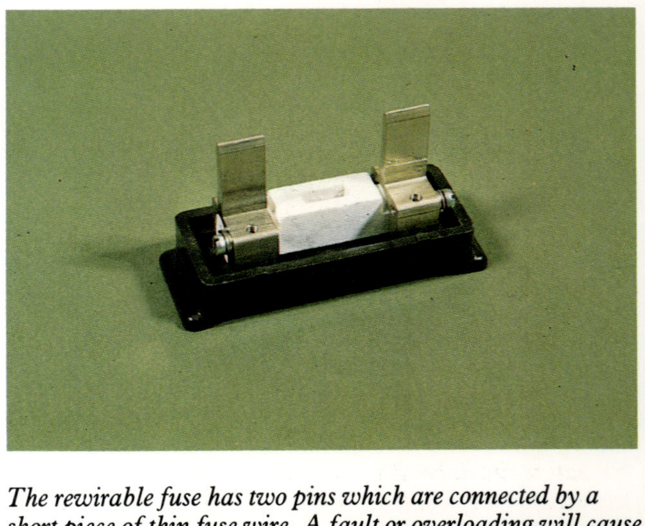

The rewirable fuse has two pins which are connected by a short piece of thin fuse wire. A fault or overloading will cause this wire to overheat and break, when a new piece of the same rated wire should be fitted in its place.

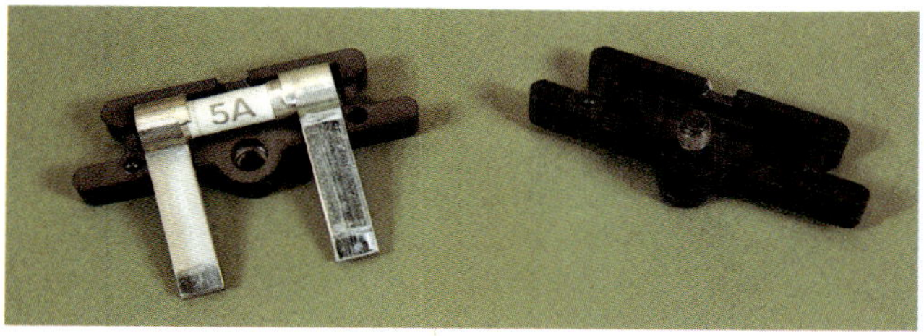

With the cartridge fuse, ratings are identified by different colours and sizes, so that when one blows it is impossible to replace it with one of a different rating. The colours are: white – 5amp; blue – 15amp; yellow – 20amp; red – 30amp; green – 45amp. You cannot repair cartridge fuses, only replace them.

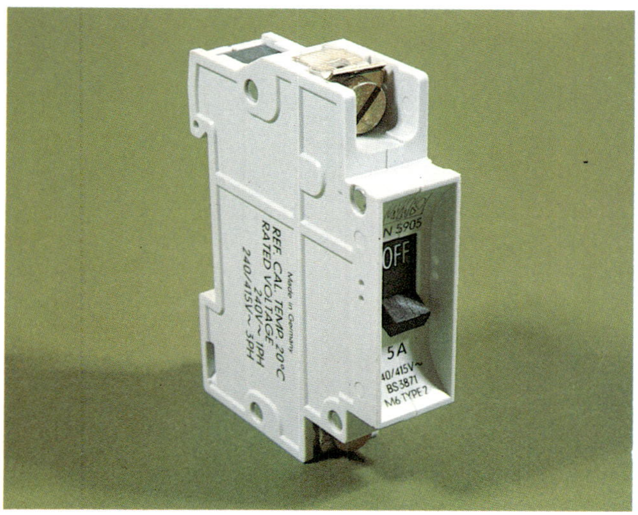

Miniature circuit breakers are more convenient than traditional fuses – but also more expensive. However, when the switch is tripped, all you need do is rectify the fault on that particular circuit and switch the miniature circuit breaker back on. Again, these are available with different ratings.

Plug fuses These cartridge fuses are fitted in all rectangular-pin plugs and in some two- or three-way adaptors. Two different ratings are available, 3 and 13amp, which are coloured red and brown respectively. These fuses protect the rest of the circuit against faults in the appliances they are used with. They cannot be repaired, but must be replaced.

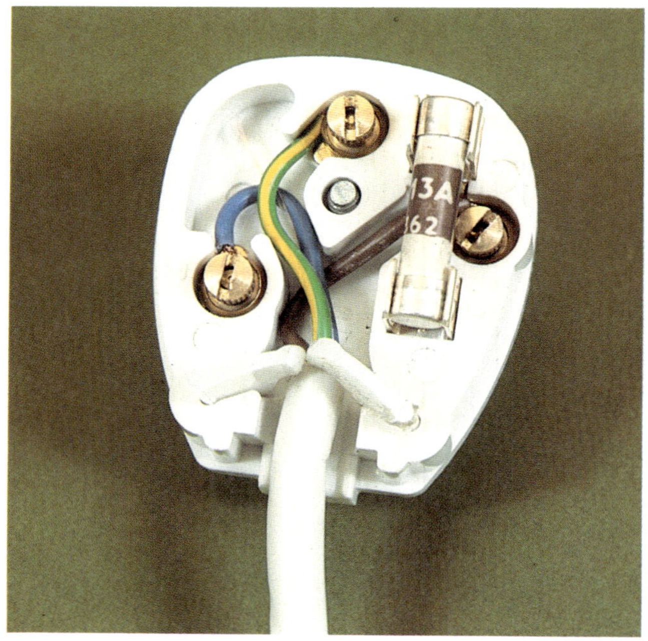

Modern plugs are fitted with cartridge fuses and these come in two ratings – 3amp (red) and 13amp (brown). Check with the manufacturer's recommendations to make sure you fit the correct fuse for the appliance. The advantage of fusing a plug is that it protects the rest of the circuit from faults that may occur within the appliance or the flex leading to it. The fuse and its carrier are always situated over the live terminal in a three-pin plug. The fuse can be levered out quite easily.

How to identify a blown fuse

Mains fuse When this type of fuse blows, no power will reach the meter or consumer unit. You can't touch it yourself and you'll have to contact the local Electricity Board.

Consumer unit fuse Switch off the power at the mains. If your fuses are of the rewirable type, pull out and check each fuse carrier. You will see a strip of thin wire between two terminals; if it is intact, the fuse is serviceable. If it has broken the fuse has blown. Often with this type of fuse you can tell which is the offending one by the blackening on the fuse. If the consumer unit is fitted with cartridge fuses, remove each cartridge fuse and check it, using the torch method (see below).

Miniature circuit breaker Inspect the row of mcbs. The one that has 'tripped' (cut off) is the one with the 'on' button sticking out.

Plug fuse There is no way of telling whether a plug cartridge fuse has blown just by looking at it, since the inside, in which the fuse wire runs, is concealed. It may be hot to touch, but this is not a

If you suspect a rewirable fuse of blowing, you can normally detect which one is affected by looking at it. Often you will see a charred mark on the carrier, but should normally see where the fuse wire has broken. This is usually in the middle, but check at either end in case it has broken there.

You will not be able to see whether a cartridge fuse has blown since the fuse wire inside is concealed. The only testing method available – apart from replacing each cartridge fuse in turn with a new one – is to use a metal-cased torch. Remove the base of the torch and hold the cartridge so that one end is touching the casing and the other the bottom of the battery. If the torch fails to work – and the bulb and batteries are sound – then the fuse has blown.

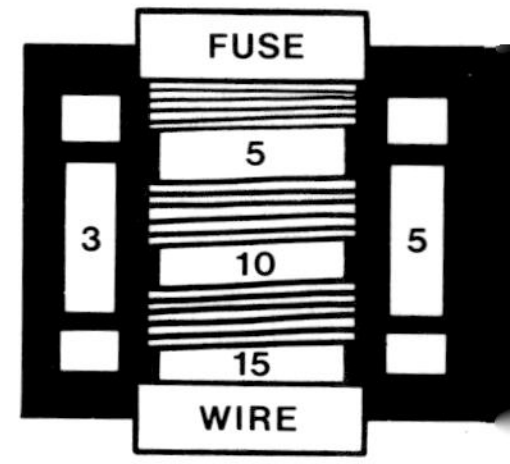

reliable guide as to whether the fuse has blown or not. Replacement with a sound fuse is the only way of telling whether the original is faulty or not, unless you use the torch method (see diagram left). When you replace a cartridge fuse check that the rating is correct for the appliance involved. A 3amp cartridge fuse can handle about 750 watts, so any appliance with a lower wattage than this should be fitted with a 3amp cartridge. Anything above 750 watts must have a 13amp fuse – as do some motorised appliances below 750 watts. The wattage is always stated on the appliance.

What causes a fuse to blow?

The reason a fuse blows is that too high a current is trying to pass through it; as it does, the wire melts and the circuit is broken. Sometimes a fuse will fail after a long period due to continuous high current usage. One particular example of this is the 13amp cartridge fuse in a plug on the end of a washing machine with a 3kW rating. In this case all you have to do is replace the fuse.

Most often, however, a fuse blows because somewhere there is a short circuit. The most common causes of a blown fuse (in order of probability) are as follows:

1. Too many appliances on one socket outlet or too many multi-way adaptors in use.
2. Too many appliances in use on one fused circuit.
3. Too many lights in use on one fused circuit.
4. Plugs have been pulled out of the socket by the flex and the connection in the plug is impaired.
5. Damaged or worn flex to an appliance, especially where it enters or leaves the appliance or plug.
6. Faulty wiring of plugs with loose terminals or spare wires bridging terminals in the plug.
7. Internal fault in the appliance.
8. Cutting a flex or driving a nail through a cable, for example.
9. Getting water on an appliance or trying to clean it while it is still plugged in (a very dangerous habit!).

Repairing a blown fuse

In the consumer unit With the cartridge type, simply remove the offending fuse and replace it. With the rewirable type, remove the fuse carrier and unscrew and take out both pieces of old fuse wire. Thread a new strip of wire of the correct rating through the holes in the fuse carrier and wrap one turn in a clockwise direction round the screw at one end and tighten it. Then wrap the other end of wire round the other screw in the same way. You must wrap the wire round in a clockwise direction so that the wire will tighten as the screw is tightened. If you do it the other way, the wire will loosen as the screw is turned. Check that the wire is gently stretched – but not taut – between the screws. Snip off the surplus wire at either end.
Important Only use one strand of fuse wire – and make sure it is of the correct rating. Never use any other type of wire and never increase the size (rating) of the wire.
In a plug To gain access to the fuse in a plug, remove the single screw holding the plug cover in place and take off the cover. You will see the fuse in a carrier connected to the live terminal of the plug, which will be marked with an L and have the brown conductor attached to it. Lift out the blown cartridge – you may need a screwdriver to ease it out of its carrier – and press in the replacement cartridge. Screw back the plug cover.
Warning A common short-cut is to wrap a piece of aluminium foil or fuse wire around a faulty fuse to restore the circuit. This is a very dangerous practice and you must never do it.

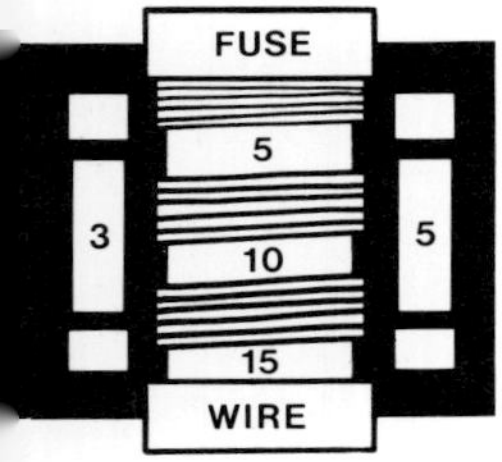

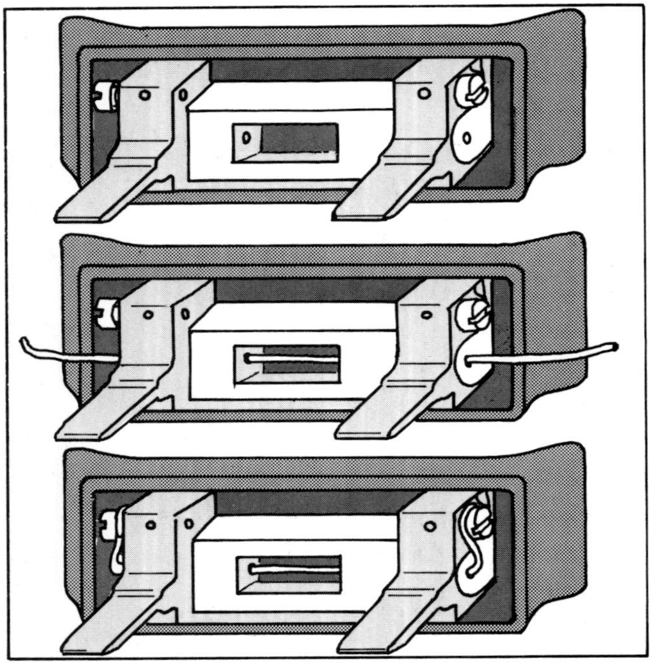

To repair a rewirable fuse, loosen the screws that hold the fuse wire in place and remove the old bits of wire. Cut off a length of new fuse wire of the correct rating for that circuit and wind each end round the relevant screw in a clockwise direction. This is important so that the wire tightens as you tighten the screw. Check there is no slack in the wire and then trim off the excess at either end so there are no bits of trailing wire.

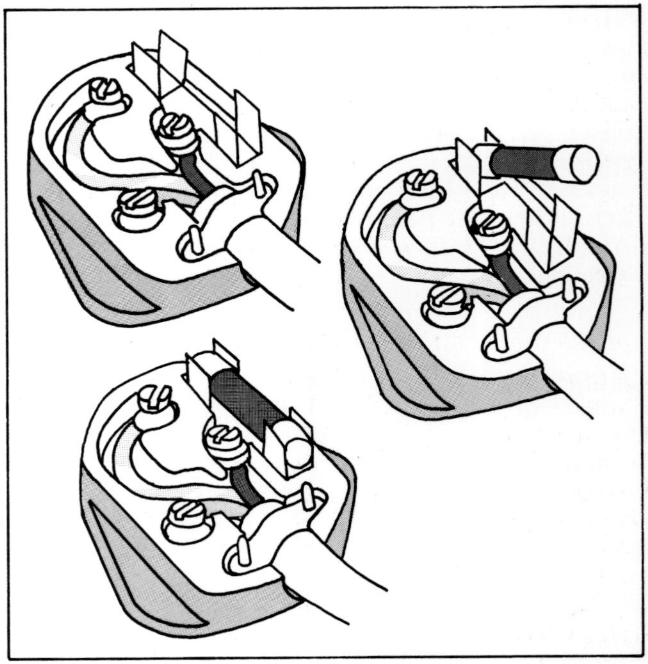

Where you suspect a blown cartridge fuse in a plug, take off the plug cover by undoing the retaining screw. Lift out the fuse, which is located over the live terminal; you may need a screwdriver to help you ease this out. Simply slot back in a new fuse of the same rating. Before you replace the cover, check that the connections to each terminal are tight and that the cord grip is firmly holding the flex as it enters the plug.

Never be tempted to wrap aluminium foil round a blown cartridge fuse. This is a very dangerous practice since you have bypassed the safety function – that is, the fuse – and removed one way of telling whether there is a fault in the circuit.

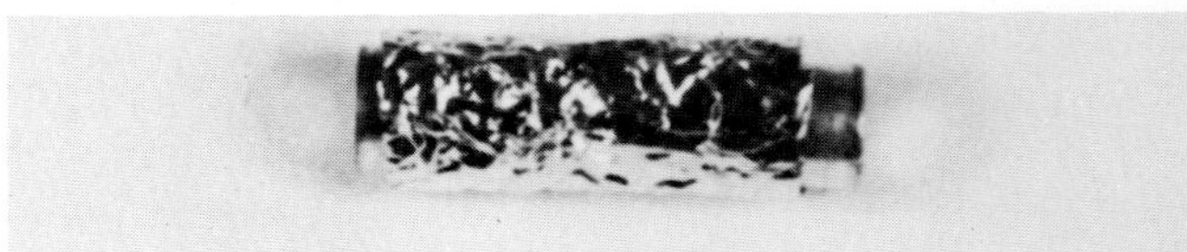

With the earth pin (the largest pin) on a metal-cased battery, there should be no possibility of the torch bulb lighting when either of the other two pins touch the side of the torch. If it does, there is a fault in the appliance which must be corrected before it is used. Continuity of a simple circuit can be checked by placing one of the two smaller pins on the battery and the other on the side of the torch with the appliance switched on. The torch bulb will light up but may well be very dim. This latter check will not work on any appliance using electronic components.

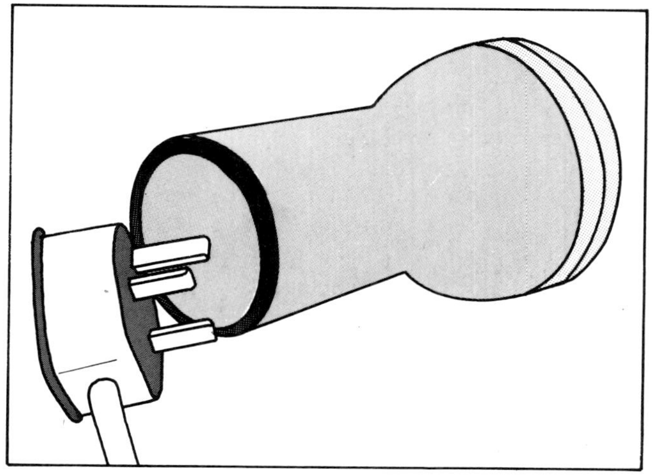

Cartridge fuse rating for 13 amp plugs

Appliance	*Wattage*	*Fuse Rating*
Blanket	120	3
Dishwasher	3000	13
Food mixer	400	3
Freezer	300	3
Hair dryer	350	3
Iron	750–1250	13
Lamp	100	3
Radio	100	3
Refrigerator	200	3
Spin dryer	300*	3
Hi-fi	125	3
TV	350*	3
Tumble dryer	2500	13
Vacuum cleaner	500*	3
Washing machine	3000	13

*Some makes of these appliances need a higher starting current than the normal running current. In these cases a 13amp fuse may be necessary. Always check with the manufacturer's instructions.

Checking faulty appliances

The most common fault with appliances, particularly those that are portable, is a worn or damaged flex or connections. Having unplugged the appliance, check the connections in both the plug and, if accessible, the appliance.

Check the appliance for blockages. In the case of an electric toaster, for example, there could be a piece of crust caught inside. In a washing machine or spin dryer socks or handkerchiefs, for example, may be jamming the drum. Check for leaks in any machine that carries water.

You can check whether there is a leak to earth by using the torch method (see page 36). This will also determine whether the circuit is broken. If you discover either of these faults, call in a qualified electrician or contact the suppliers.

Fault finding in the lighting circuit

(Permanently wired-in lights)

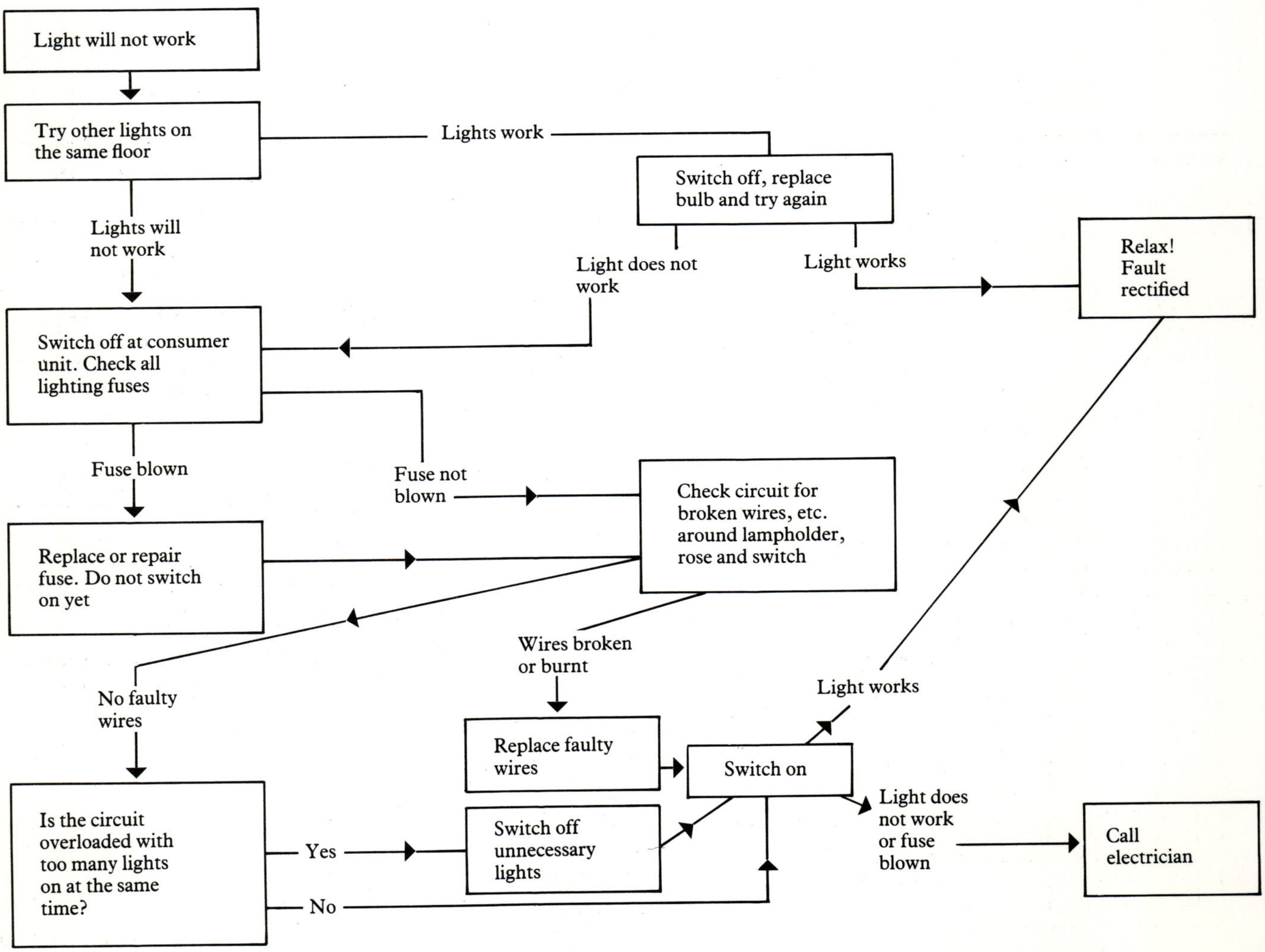

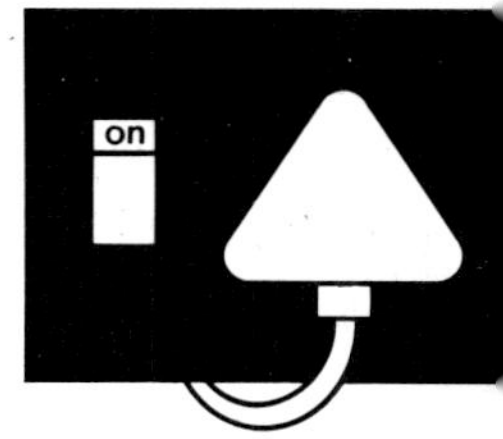

Fault finding in the power circuit

(Appliance from a three-pin plug)

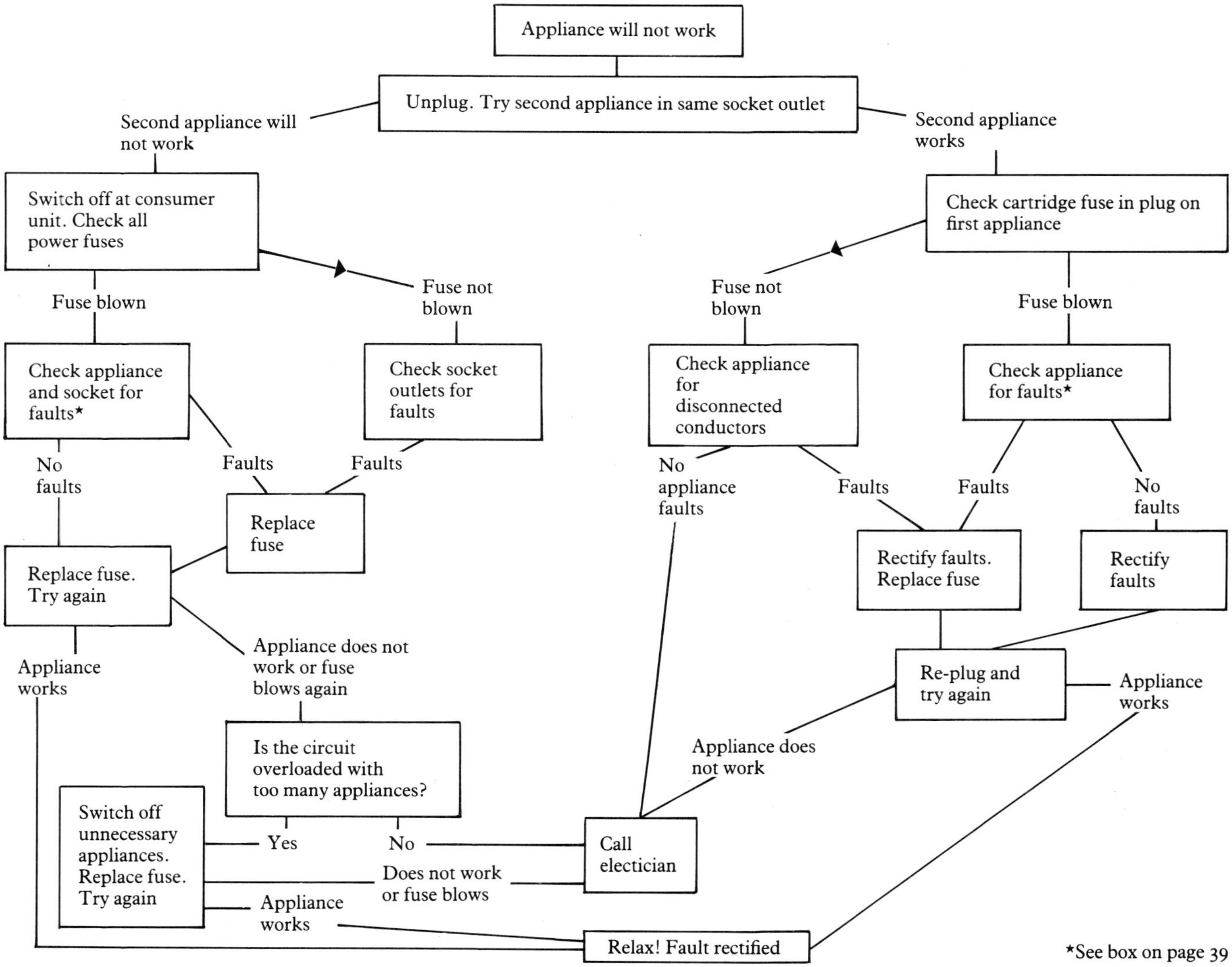

*See box on page 39

5 Cables and flexes

A cable contains a set of conductors usually having solid or heavy stranded cores used for permanent connections in the wiring installation. It is flexible enough to be bent into place, but once installed would not be expected to move again. A flex contains a set of conductors used for connecting an appliance to a power outlet or a lampholder to a ceiling rose. As the name implies, it is flexible and can be twisted and bent (within reason) to allow any portable appliance to be moved about.

Types of cable

Modern cables have an outer covering of PVC, which is damp and rot-proof. Within this outer cover are two main conductors; these are also encased in PVC. One is coloured red and is the live conductor; the other is coloured black and is the neutral conductor.

There is a separate bare copper wire, usually slightly smaller than the other two, running inside the outer casing. This is the earth conductor and is there to provide a continuous path to earth in the event of an electrical fault in the installation or appliance. Normally when the current flows through this wire a fuse blows immediately.

In older houses cables may be of a single core running in a steel conduit or lead- or rubber-covered two- or three-core cable. All of these are subject to deterioration and should be replaced. This involves the rewiring of all circuits in the home and you should consult a qualified electrician to tackle this job.

For use in outdoor locations, special cables are available. These come in two types.

Mineral insulated copper-sheathed cable has two conductors coated with PVC and surrounded by mineral insulation inside a copper tube, which has a thin PVC sleeve over it. This cable needs special joints at the ends. The other type has a steel wire sleeve surrounding the conductors. In both types, the outer metal casing is used as the earth return. Any work using these types of cable should be left to a qualified electrician.

The above-mentioned cables are available with varying sizes of conductors. The current load is the determining factor in deciding which size of cable to use. This table below shows some of the sizes used in the home.

Conductor size (sq mm)	*Current rating (amp) using cartridge fuses*	*Normal use*
1.0	14	Lighting circuits
1.5	18	Lighting and radial circuits
2.5	24	Ring main power circuits
4.0	32	Cooker circuit
6.0	40	Large size cooker circuit, consumer unit to meter

Types of flex

With flexes, the conductors are made from many thin strands twisted together rather than the single conductors you find in cables. This enables flex to be bent many times and twisted. Continuous bending and twisting will, however, cause wear and flex will need replacing from time to time if it gets much of this kind of treatment. This is particularly so with, for example, the flex on an iron or vacuum cleaner.

Flexes are available in two- or three-core PVC, rubber or textile braided covering. The modern colour codings are different from those of cable – with the live conductor coloured brown, the neutral blue and the earth green and yellow. Old flexes will be coloured red, black and green respectively, but you will not find these colours on new flexes.

The flex often used for irons and kettles is rubber-insulated and textile braided. The textile is woven around the three conductors and several strands of textile fillers to make up a circular flex. When the flex is fitted, you must take care to prevent the textile braiding unravelling.

Two- and three-core PVC-sheathed flexes are available for all appliances. The PVC gives a water-resistant and easy-to-clean finish. You can get a special orange-coloured PVC-sheathed flex for electrically operated outdoor tools. The colour has been designed to stand out clearly and help prevent the possibility of the flex being accidentally cut. When buying two-core flex, you must ensure that it is designed for full mains voltage, since you can get cheaper low voltage flex for connecting items such as doorbells. This could be dangerous because the conductors are liable to overheat and lead to fire hazards.

The old-fashioned twisted two-core flex is now virtually obsolete.

All double-insulated appliances, however, should always be fitted with a colour-coded two-core flex.

One of the main reasons for flex failure is that the ends are not secured correctly. All plugs and appliances are fitted with some device to hold the flex firmly in place to avoid strain in the terminal connections. This grip should always be properly adjusted.

Different sizes of flex are obtainable to suit the current rating required. Always check that the flex can handle the full current needed by the appliance and is protected by the correct-sized fuse in the plug.

Rating for flexes

Size (sq mm)	*Current rating (amps)*	*Appliance/rating (watts)*
0.5	3	Light fitting up to 100 watts
0.75	6	Light fitting/small appliance
1.0	10	Up to 2000 watts
1.25	13	Up to 3000 watts
1.5	15	Up to 3600 watts

Refer to illustration on page 45.

1. Twin-core single insulated cable – this light duty cable is not colour-coded and is designed for lighting and bell circuit installations.

2. Twin-core and earth double insulated cable – this is colour-coded and designed (in various sizes) for most cable runs through the home. The red conductor is live, the black neutral and the bare earth.

3. Three-core and earth double insulated cable – this is colour-coded differently for identification purposes and has no significance for home wiring. It is used for two and three-way switching circuits and the colour coding for the current-carrying conductors is red, yellow and blue, with earth bare.

4. Heavy-duty two-core and earth double insulated cable – here the colour coding is as usual, but each of the live and neutral conductors is made up of several twisted strands.

5. Four-core copper sheathed and mineral insulated cable – this is used for outdoor wiring. The special end fitting is put on by the supplier.

Refer to illustration on page 46.

1. Three-core textile-braided and rubber insulated flex – this carries the standard colour coding of brown for live, blue for neutral and green/yellow for earth. It is used mainly with irons and kettles since it is more resistant to wear when it rubs against work surfaces.

2. Three-core rubber covered and insulated flex – this carries the standard colour coding and, with PVC covered flex, is the most common type used.

3. Three-core PVC covered and insulated flex – it carries the standard colour coding and is the most commonly used flex in the home.

4. Two-core PVC covered and insulated flex – this is colour-coded for the live and neutral conductors, but carries no earth conductor. It is used with double-insulated appliances that are plugged in to a normal power socket outlet.

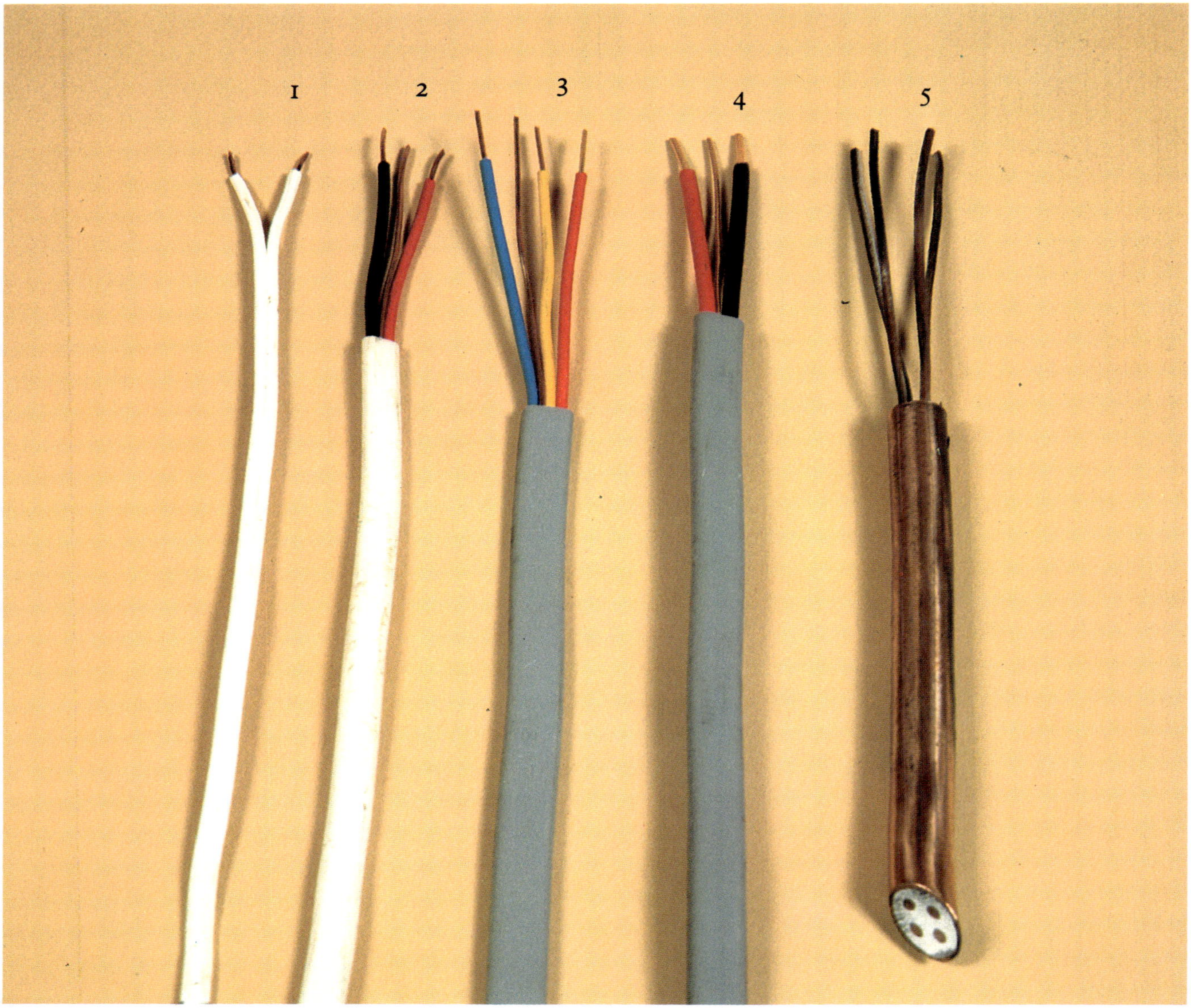
1
2
3
4
5

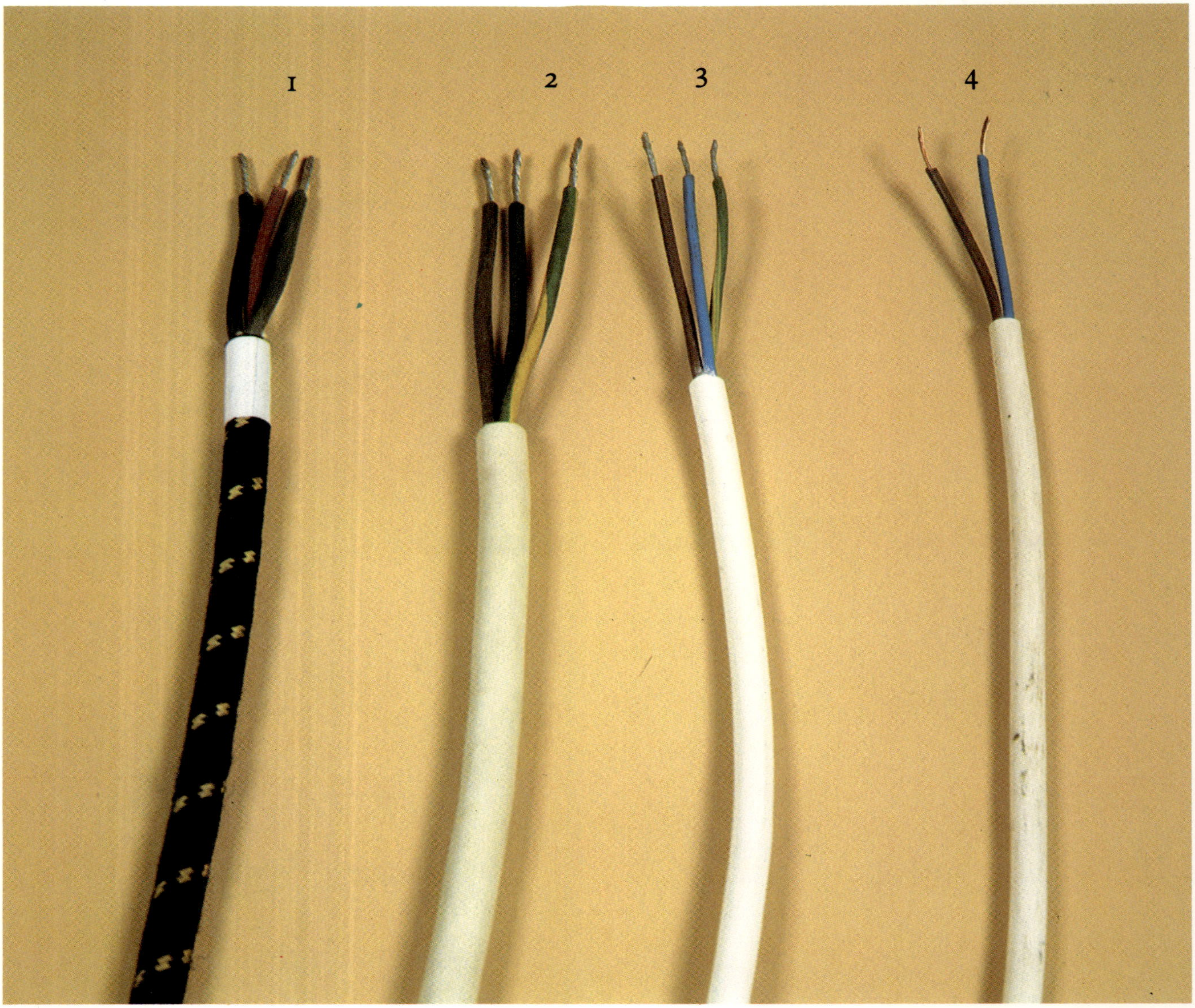
1
2
3
4

6 Plugs and how to wire them

Types of plug

In old houses two-pin plugs were traditionally used; these had round pins and carried ratings of 2amp or 5amp. If still in use, these should only be used for insulated lights or double-insulated appliances.

The one modern appliance carrying a two-pin plug is the electric shaver, which has a very low current rating – and, incidentally, can be connected up and used in a bathroom for that reason but only via a special shaver socket with an isolating transformer.

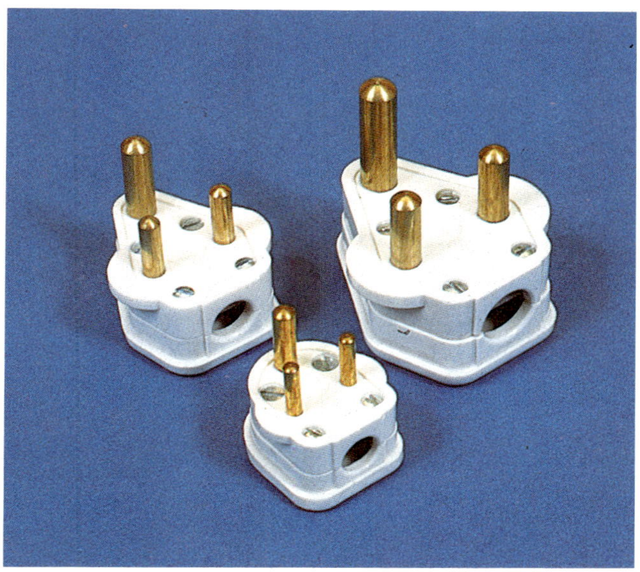

The range of traditional round-pin plugs includes those rated at 2amp (for lamps), 5amp (for appliances up to 1kW) and 15amp (for appliances up to 3kW). None of these plugs is fused.

The round three-pin plugs are also traditional in older houses. There are two sizes available – with 5amp and 15amp ratings. No fuses are fitted to these plugs.

The modern plug has three rectangular pins with a maximum rated capacity of 13amp. It is fitted with a fuse of 3amp or 13amp capacity depending on the type of appliance to which it is fitted. On some plugs the pins are insulated on the top half of their length. This prevents the possibility of the person handling them getting a shock when inserting the plug into a live socket outlet.

Plugs are available at various prices. Always try to use good plugs (to BS 1363). When wiring up a

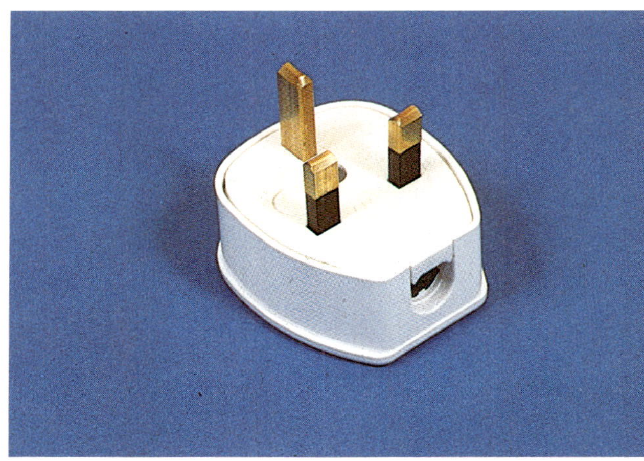

A modern rectangular-pin plug with a maximum rated capacity of 13amp. Depending on the type of appliance used, it should contain either a 3amp or 13amp fuse. There is a range of plugs available and the only safe guide is to buy the more expensive, better quality plugs – particularly for use with high rated appliances. Plugs with insulated pins offer additional safety when inserting or removing from a socket – and should always be used with an unswitched socket.

washing machine or a similar heavily loaded appliance, the more expensive plug should be fitted to prevent the socket outlet and plug overheating.

Plugs are normally available in plastic, but you can buy special rubberised versions for appliances subjected to rough treatment, such as those for outdoor use. Special waterproof plugs and socket outlets are available too.

All these plugs are fitted with a cord-grip of some type, which must always be correctly adjusted to hold the flex firmly in the plug and prevent the conductors pulling away from their terminals.

Low voltage (110v) plugs with three rectangular pins are also available. With these the pins are twisted 90 degrees from the normal mains voltage plugs to make it impossible to fit a low voltage appliance into a mains socket or vice-versa.

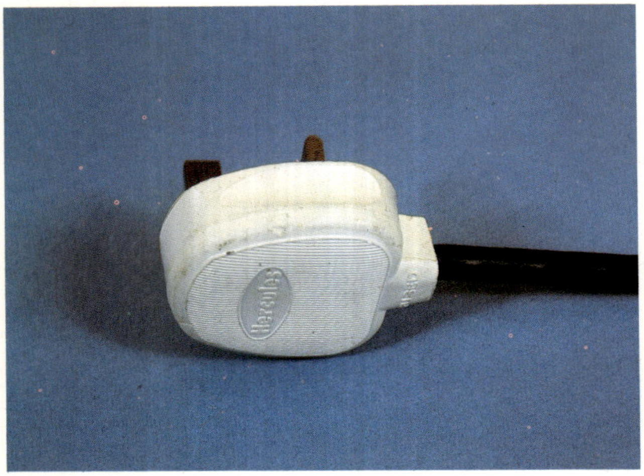

Rubberised plugs should be fitted onto appliances that undergo heavy wear and tear and are likely to be dropped onto hard surfaces – such as the concrete floor of a workshop or garage. This will avoid the possibility of the plug being cracked, which could be dangerous.

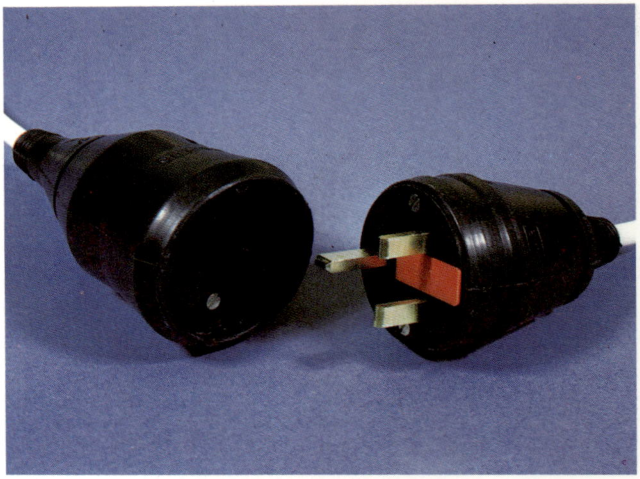

Waterproof plugs and sockets are for use outdoors, and their value is obvious. They are available with a screw-on cap to prevent water getting inside.

Special plugs are available for use in 110v circuits. The pins are twisted through 180° to prevent low voltage appliances being accidentally plugged into a circuit with normal mains voltage (240v). Some plugs have both the live and neutral terminals fused.

Plug adaptors

There are various types of adaptor available to enable you to run two or more fittings or appliances from one socket outlet. You can also buy adaptors that allow you to use round-pin plugs via a 13amp socket outlet, which of course is designed to take rectangular-pin plugs.

You will find the better quality adaptors incorporate a fuse. These are much safer to use since the fuse in the adaptor prevents you from accidentally overloading the socket outlet.

You should always remember that the maximum loading on one socket outlet is 13amps and you should never use an adaptor to operate more than one fitting or appliance if the total loading when they are switched on exceeds this. Their use should be restricted to, for example, a hi-fi deck and an amplifier, which for convenience can be run together off one socket outlet, or possibly a television and a table lamp.

It is a very dangerous practice to use more than one adaptor in any one socket outlet simply to provide the facility for extra plugs.

A smaller adaptor is also available to enable you to plug in an electric shaver into a 13amp socket outlet. But remember that this type of outlet must never be fitted or used in a bathroom, where there should never be any exposed socket outlets – except that designed specifically to take an electric shaver.

There are various types of two and three-way adaptors available, and you can use them either to increase the number of outlets from a single socket or to convert a round-pin socket outlet to take rectangular-pin plugs (or vice-versa). Those with in-built fuses are preferable, particularly when making the round-pin conversion. Never use more than one adaptor from any one socket outlet.

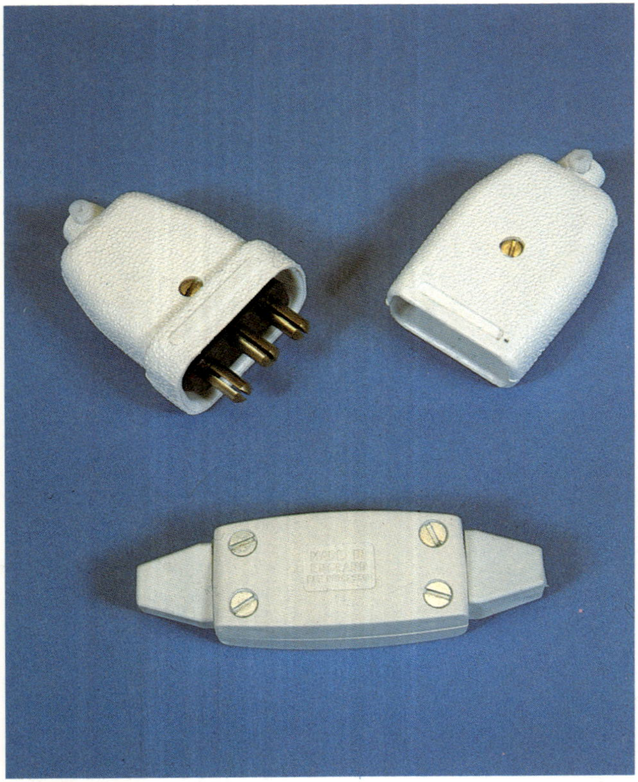

Flex connectors are available as a single unit and in detachable two and three-pin versions. Bearing in mind that it is not recommended to join flex, these should only be used where absolutely necessary – for example, as an extension to a flex where the length of flex required would be unmanageable in terms of storage, etc. Remember that, when wiring up a detachable connector, the flex from the appliance should be wired to the male (pin) section of the connector and the flex to the plug wired to the female socket section. If the connector becomes detached while the current is still switched on, you will not run the risk of getting an electric shock by touching 'live' pins.

Types of flex connector

Flex connectors, which are available as a single fixed unit and also in detachable two- and three-pin versions, are used as a means of extending a flex. However, it is always safer and preferable to have the correct or desired length of flex in the first place – or to install a new socket outlet nearer the place of work to avoid the need for long, trailing flexes. In any case, remember you must never try to join lengths of flex by twisting corresponding conductors together and taping them up. When using a detachable flex connector, it should always have the same number of pins as the flex has conductors.

ALWAYS connect the pin (male) end of a connector to the flex leading to the appliance and the socket (female) end to the flex leading to the socket. There is a very good reason for this. If by any chance the flex connector comes apart and the male end is the one joined to the flex leading to the socket, the pins will be live – and therefore dangerous.

Stripping conductors

This involves exposing the bare conductors at the end of a cable or flex to enable a connection to be made to the terminals of a plug or socket. It is most important to ensure that you expose only the correct amount of conductor and that you do not damage the core insulation when you cut back the outer covering. You must also make sure that you do not cut into the conductors when you cut through the core insulation, since this will reduce the current-carrying capacity of the cable or flex and cause the connection to overheat.

The best and safest way to strip the insulation off conductors is to use one of the many types of wire strippers. You can use pliers or a sharp knife, but with these you have less control over the cutting and the chances of damaging the conductor are that much greater.

First remove about 40mm (or 1½in) of the outer covering. This operation is best done with a sharp knife – the one time when you can use this tool. But take extra care not to cut into the core insulation, or worse still, right through into the conductors themselves.

If the flex is textile-braided, wrap a piece of PVC insulation tape around the flex where you are making the cut; this will prevent the cloth from unravelling. You can get rubber sleeving for this.

With PVC insulation, make one cut along the outer covering, open it out, double it back down and cut off the waste.

Set the wire strippers so that the cutter leaves a hole just big enough for the conductor to pass through. Pinch the handles together and cut the core insulation about 15mm (⅝in) from the end, rotating the strippers half a turn. Give the strippers a sharp pull and the unwanted insulation will slide off. Tidy up the strands of the conductor by twisting them tightly together. Loose or stray strands could cause a short circuit in the plug if they accidentally touch other bare strands or terminals.

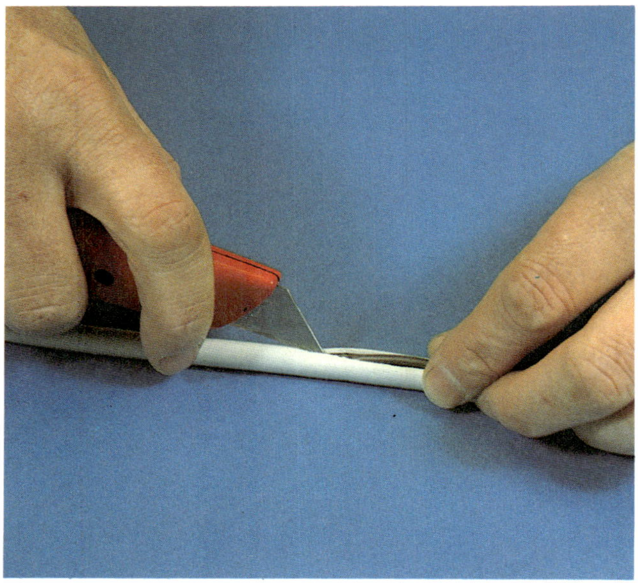

When preparing the end of a length of cable or flex for connection to the relevant set of terminals, first strip back the outer insulation by making a single cut of about 40mm (1½in). Take care here not to damage the insulated conductors.

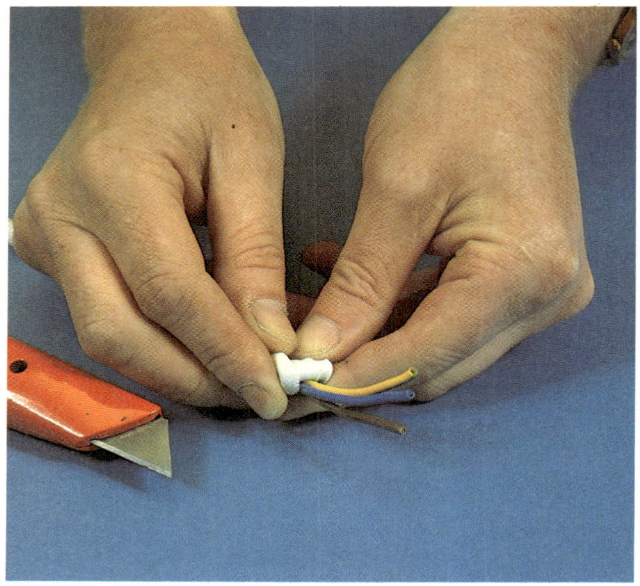

Bend back the outer insulation and carefully trim it off along the fold. Use a sharp knife to cut off the waste, but make sure you do not damage any of the insulation on the conductors. The safest way is to hold the end of the cable or flex in one hand and cut away.

Make sure you have not cut off any of the strands. If you have, you will have to remove the exposed section of cable or flex and start all over again. This is not only time-wasting but also shortens the cable or flex – and if you have estimated exactly the right length, this will be very inconvenient. It is always best to allow an extra 50mm (2in) or so in the length in case you make a mistake.

With terminal block connections, dip the ends into solder paste and melt the solder with a suitable flame – from, for example, a cigarette lighter – to solder all the strands neatly together. This will give you the best connection. Take great care when applying the flame not to burn the conductor insulation.

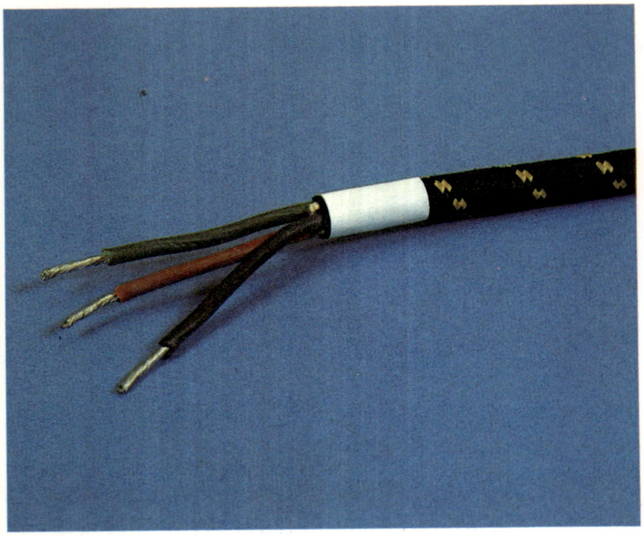

If your flex is textile-braided, you should wrap insulation tape around the cut end to prevent fraying. You can get rubber sleeving to slip over the cut end which will have the same effect.

When working with small flex, since the conductors are quite thin, you will get the best connection with the terminals by bending back and doubling the twisted ends. This enables the terminal screw to bite better on the conductor. When stripping cable, because of the thickness of the conductors, you will have to use pliers to twist the stranded ends tightly together.

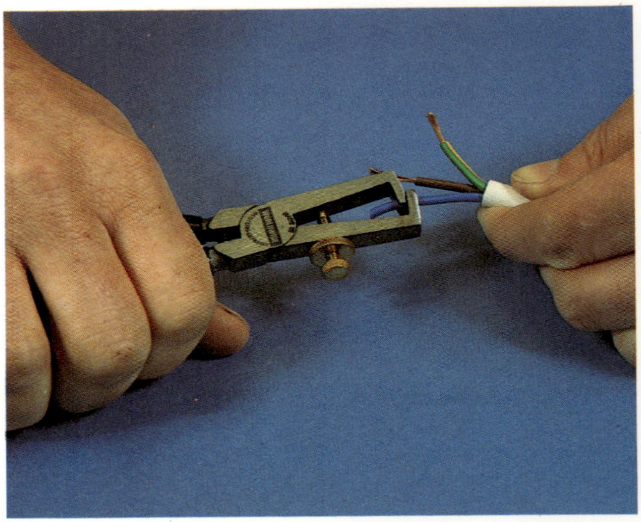

The adjustment on wire strippers varies according to the type. But the rule is that the conductor should just slide into the set hole in the strippers. To save making any mistakes, it is a good idea to practise with a scrap length of flex or cable identical to the one on which you are working.

The safest way of stripping the insulation off each conductor is to use wire strippers. Set these for the correct diameter of each conductor and squeeze the handles to cut off the insulation – about 15mm (5/8in) from the end – rotating the strippers about half a turn. Give the strippers a hard pull and the insulation should slide off the conductor.

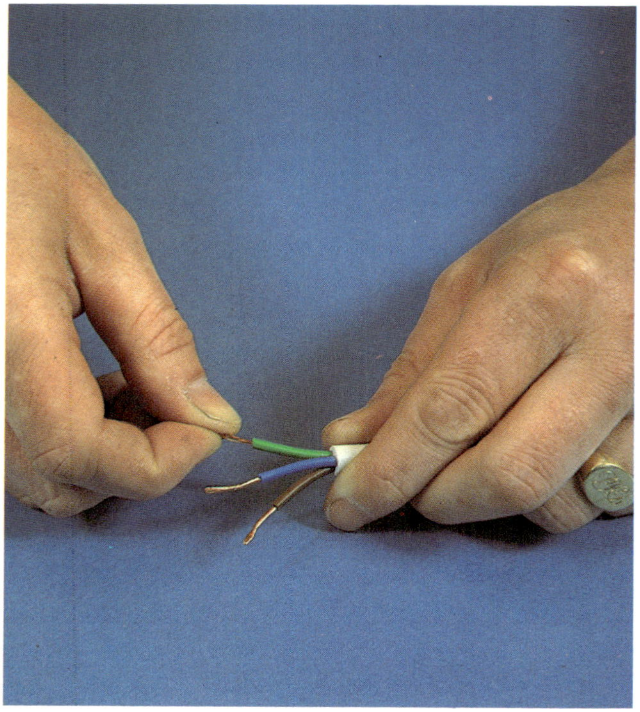

To ensure a good connection when the exposed end of each conductor is inserted into the relevant terminal, twist the strands of wire tightly together with your fingers. Loose or stray strands will not only make the conduction of electricity less efficient but may cause a short circuit if they should accidentally touch loose strands from another conductor – or another terminal. When working with heavy duty cable, you will probably have to twist the strands together with a pair of pliers to ensure that you have neat ends.

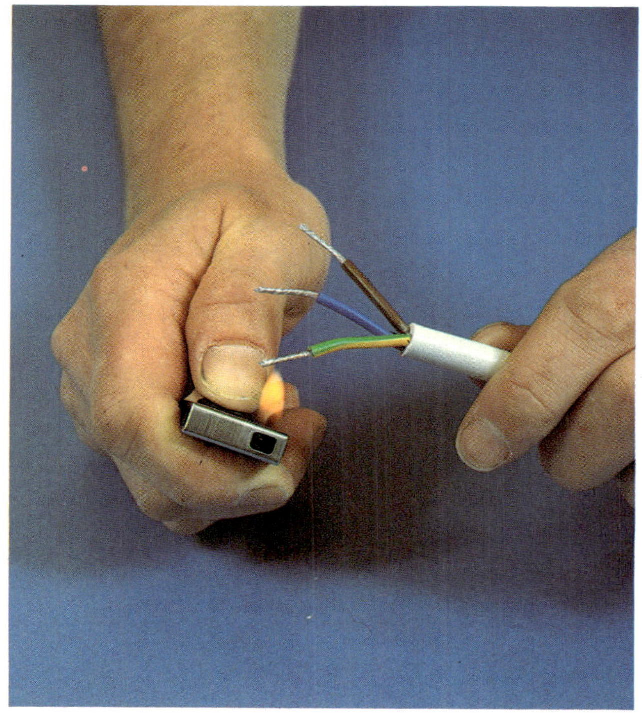

The best method to tidy off the cut end of a conductor is to solder the strands together. Tidy up any loose strands and then dip the end into solder paste. Then apply heat to melt the solder, which will fuse the loose strands together. The flame from a cigarette lighter is ideal. Make sure when you apply the heat that the flame does not touch the insulation. With very thin flex, you will get the best results by bending back the bared ends of each conductor to ensure a good connection when secured to the terminal.

Wiring up a three-pin plug

Having prepared the end of the flex for connection to the plug by stripping the conductors as described, remove the large retaining screw, which is normally located between the pins, and remove the top of the plug. Before you try to insert the end of the flex, you will have to loosen the cord-grip screws to enable you to feed the flex into the plug. Then loosen the screws in each terminal to give you room to insert the relevant conductors into each one.

With some of the cheaper plugs, the pins may fall out when you turn the plug over, so be prepared for this. You should find a fuse in the carrier over the live terminal. Depending on the type of plug, you may have to lift this out before making the necessary connections. You may find the fuse will need some persuasion and the blade of a screwdriver is ideal to help it out of its carrier.

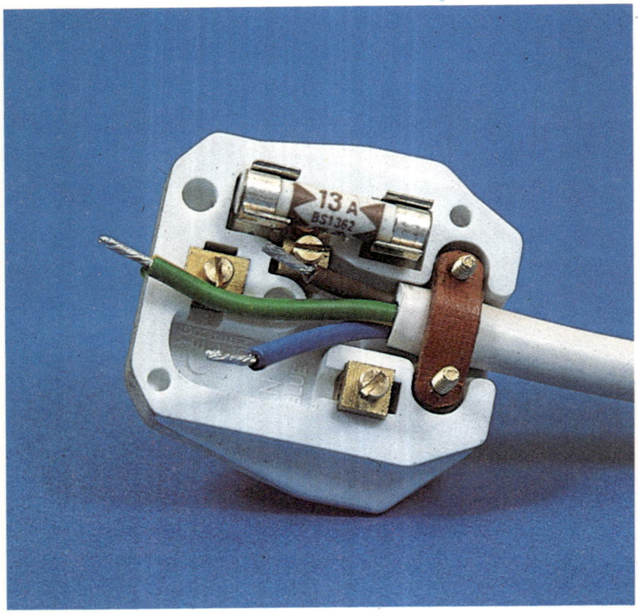

When wiring up a plug, remove the cover by releasing the retaining screw, loosen the cord grip and feed through the end of the flex, making sure that at least 3mm (1/8in) of the outer insulation is inside the plug, onto which the cord grip will tighten. Now check that the earth conductor reaches the earth terminal and tighten the cord grip to hold the flex in the plug.

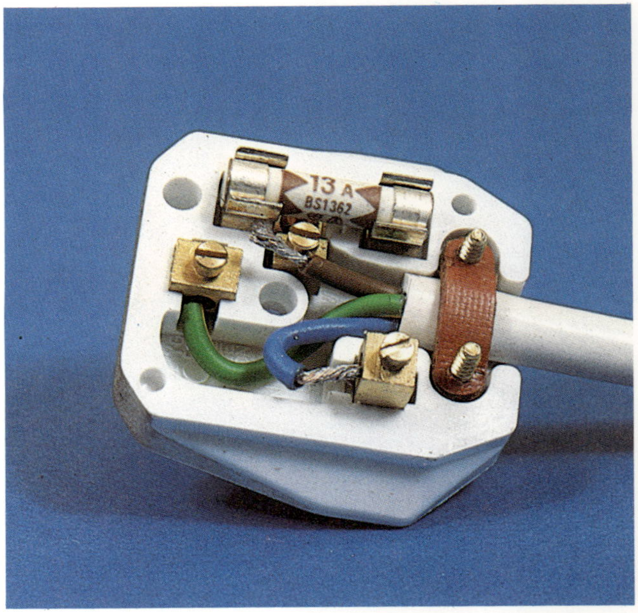

Having trimmed each conductor to 6mm (1/4in) beyond its relevant terminal, strip off 15mm (5/8in) of insulation from each conductor in turn and prepare the ends (see pages 51-53). Then release the screw in the earth terminal, insert the end of the green/yellow conductor and tighten the screw. Ensure the connection is tight and then move to the neutral terminal.

Thread the flex through the cord-grip and twist the flex so that the brown-coloured connector is on the right (by the terminal marked L), the blue on the left (by the terminal marked N) and the green and yellow in the middle (near the E terminal).

It is important that you make sure at least 3mm (⅛in) of the outer covering of the flex is inside the plug, since the cord-grip, when tightened, must secure this covering – not the individual conductors, which could otherwise be damaged. This will ensure that the flex is firmly gripped in the plug and should not put stress on the connections if the flex is stretched or pulled through use.

Check that the green and yellow conductor reaches the earth terminal comfortably and will not be stretched when connected. Bend each of the three conductors as required to their relevant terminals – brown to the live (L) terminal, blue to the neutral (N) terminal and green and yellow to the earth (E) terminal.

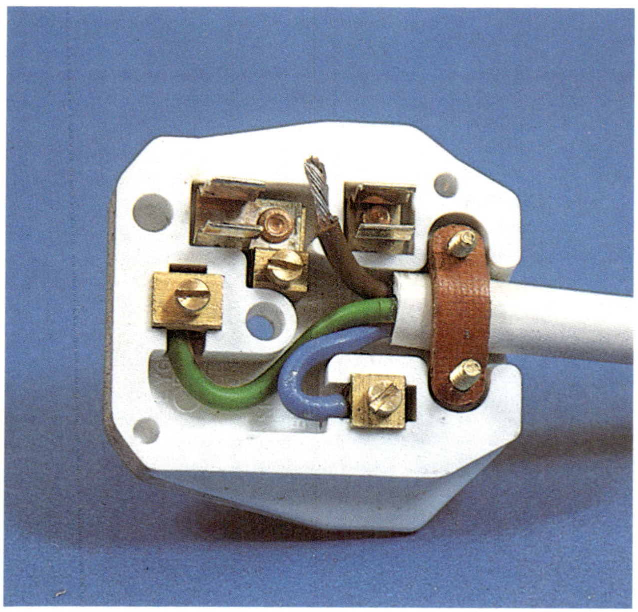

Connect up the blue conductor to the neutral (left-hand) terminal in the same way and then remove the fuse from the live (right-hand) terminal. Depending on the type of plug you are wiring, you may be able to connect up the live terminal without removing the fuse.

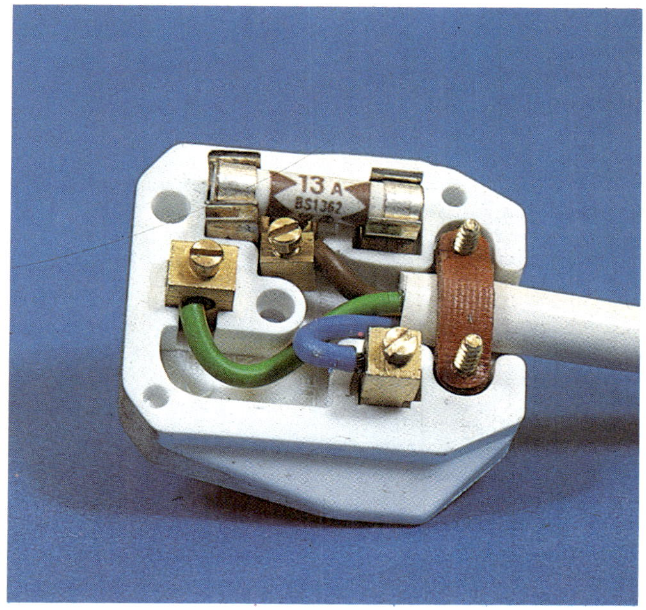

Connect up the brown conductor to the live terminal and then replace the fuse, checking that it is of the recommended rating for the appliance being used. Having checked all the connections, making sure the correct conductor goes to the correct terminal, screw back the cover.

When you have found out the exact length you want for each conductor, trim each one 6mm (¼in) beyond the terminal block. Work on the green and yellow conductor first, since this will need to be longer than the other two conductors.

Having cut each conductor to the length required, strip back the core insulation 15mm (⅝in) from the end with wire strippers. Take care not to damage any of the strands of wire. When you have taken off the insulation, twist each conductor to ensure there are no stray strands left loose.

If your plug has terminal block connections, double back the bared end of the conductor and feed it into the hole in the side of the terminal block. When the bare end has been inserted, tighten the terminal screw on the top of the block to ensure the conductor inside is gripped securely.

If your plug has clamp-type terminals, wrap the bare end of the conductor around the terminal post in a clockwise direction and then secure it by tightening the terminal screw. Don't wrap the conductor round in an anti-clockwise direction. As

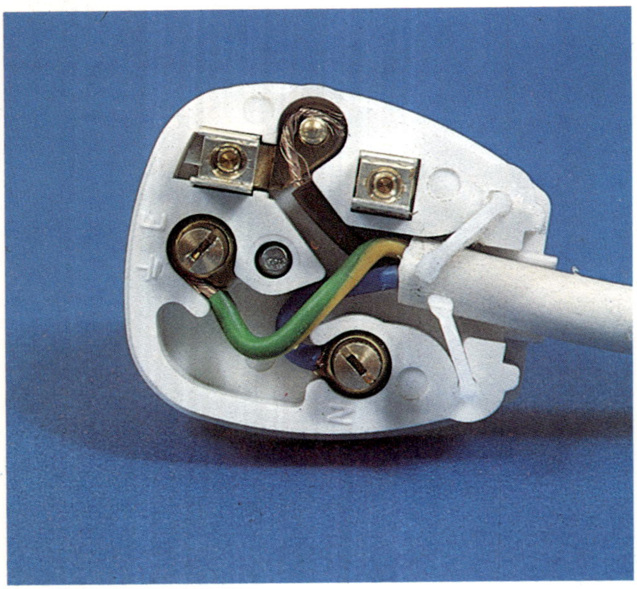

Some plugs are fitted with clamp-type terminals. Although the procedure for preparing the ends of each conductor are as before, the conductors are wrapped round the terminal post and not inserted through a hole in the terminal. Make sure you wrap the end of each conductor clockwise round the post so that it is tightened into the post when the terminal screw is tightened.

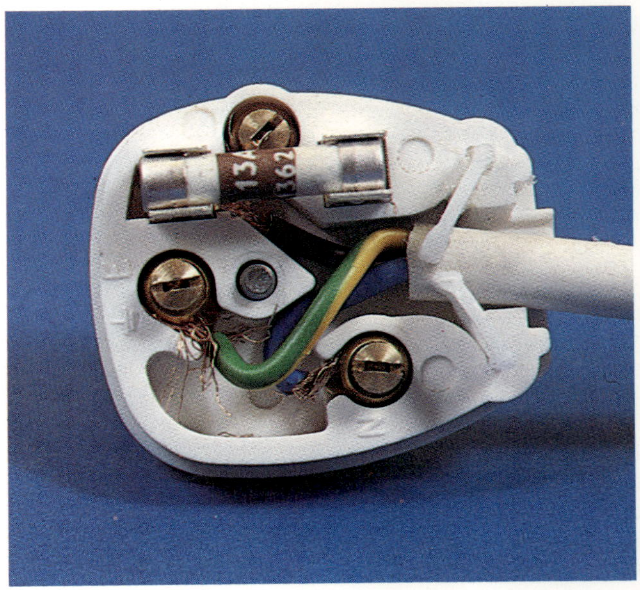

With the clamp-type terminal, it is even more advisable to neaten the ends of each conductor, since otherwise there is more chance of leaving whiskers of the conductor exposed – and these could cause a short circuit or earth fault if they touch other live parts in the plug. Overheating could also result from the fact that there are less strands to conduct the electricity.

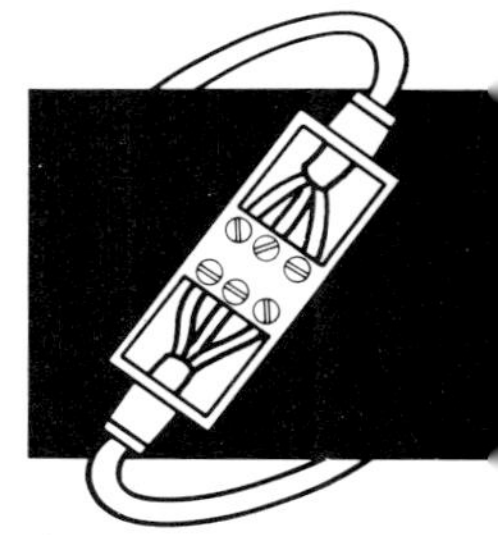

you tighten the screw, you will automatically be turning against the conductor and will force it out and away from the terminal post.

You will find with some types of plug you buy that the live terminal connection is a separate piece of metal held in place by the fuse. In other plugs it is a permanent connection underneath the fuse. Whichever type you have, the method of connection is similar.

It is very important that the connections are made correctly to ensure the safety of the plug and to allow the maximum amount of current to run through the conductors.

When each conductor is connected to its relevant terminal, the core insulation should come right up to the terminal block and you should not be able to see any bare conductors. Make sure there are no stray 'whiskers' anywhere in the plug and that the conductors lie neatly in the channels provided in the plug.

This is particularly important when you replace the plug cover, since the conductors do have a habit of rising in the plug. Make sure they are correctly positioned before you screw down the cover or you may pinch a conductor between the cover and the base of the plug.

Before you screw back the plug cover, make one final check that the correct conductors have been connected to the correct terminals, that you have the correct rate of fuse in the plug for the appliance you want to connect and that all terminal screws are tight and the connections secure. Check also the screws in the cord-grip are tight and then screw down the plug cover.

Wiring a flex connector

Flex connectors are available in two basic types, one being permanently fixed and the other being detachable, the flex being joined to separate halves which slot together like a plug to a socket.

Fixed connector To wire up this type of connector, cut back about 50mm (2in) of insulation on the ends of both flexes to be joined and strip back about 15mm (⅝in) of insulation from each conductor. Unscrew the connector cover. Slip the flexible ferrules over the ends of the flexes and feed the flex under the cord-grips at either end of the connector; the grips must secure the outer insulation. Where the flexes have earth (green and yellow) conductors, connect these to the centre terminal in the connector. The brown (live) and blue (neutral) conductors should be connected to the outer terminals. Make sure the conductors lie neatly in the connector, tighten the cord-grips and replace the cover.

Detachable connector This type of connector is normally used with appliances that need a long length of flex and is useful because the extra length can be detached and coiled up separately.

You must make sure that the flex from the appliance is fixed to the male (pin) half of the connector and the flex from the plug to the female (socket) half of the connector. If you fix the flexes the other way round – and accidentally separate the connector when the power is switched on – you could get a nasty shock if you touch the exposed pins.

To wire up this type of connector, cut back about 35mm (1½in) of the outer insulation of the flex from the appliance and strip back about 15mm (⅝in) of the insulation on each conductor. Unscrew the flex connector and slip the outer cover onto the flex. Feed the flex through the cord-grip on the male half of the connector. Connect the earth (green

and yellow) conductor to the earth (E) terminal, the live (brown) conductor to the live (L) terminal and the neutral (blue) conductor to the neutral (N) terminal. Make sure the connections are secure, tighten the cord-grip and re-fit the outer cover.

Repeat this procedure with the flex from the plug onto the female half of the flex connector.

Warning Remember that ideally you should avoid joining flex. The best solution is either to provide additional socket outlets where needed or to have longer lengths of flex fitted to the appliance. If you are using a connector for outdoor power tools, always have the connector fitted close to the tool to prevent it trailing on damp ground.

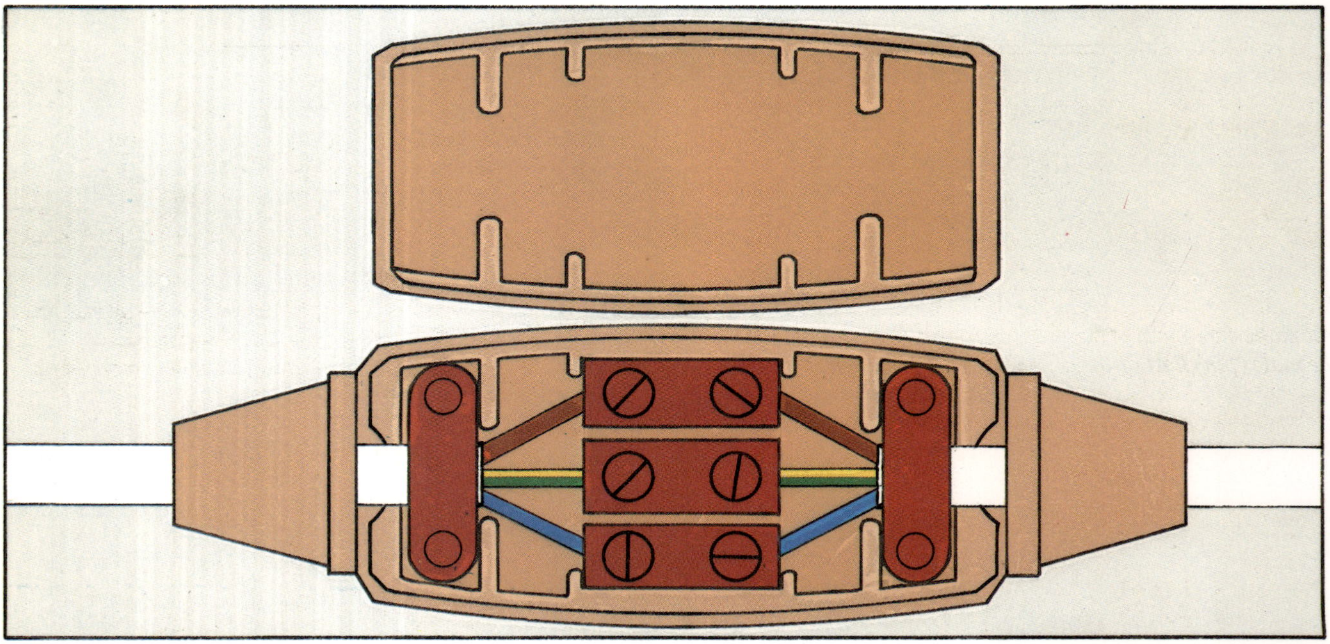

When wiring up a fixed flex connector, release the two retaining screws to remove the cover. Feed the ends of the two lengths of flex into the connector, making sure that at least 3mm (1/8in) of the outer insulation on each length is securely held in the cord grip at either end. Prepare the ends of each conductor as you would when wiring up a plug and then feed each conductor into matching terminals. This means that both live (brown) conductors must be fixed to the same terminal, equally both neutral (blue) and earth (green/yellow) conductors. Where you are using flex with an earth conductor, this should be fixed to the middle of the three terminals. It does not matter which side of this terminal the live and neutral conductors go, as long as live goes with live and neutral with neutral. Where two-core flex is not colour-coded, you can connect the conductors to either of the outside terminals. As with ordinary plugs, make sure your connections are always neat and tight.

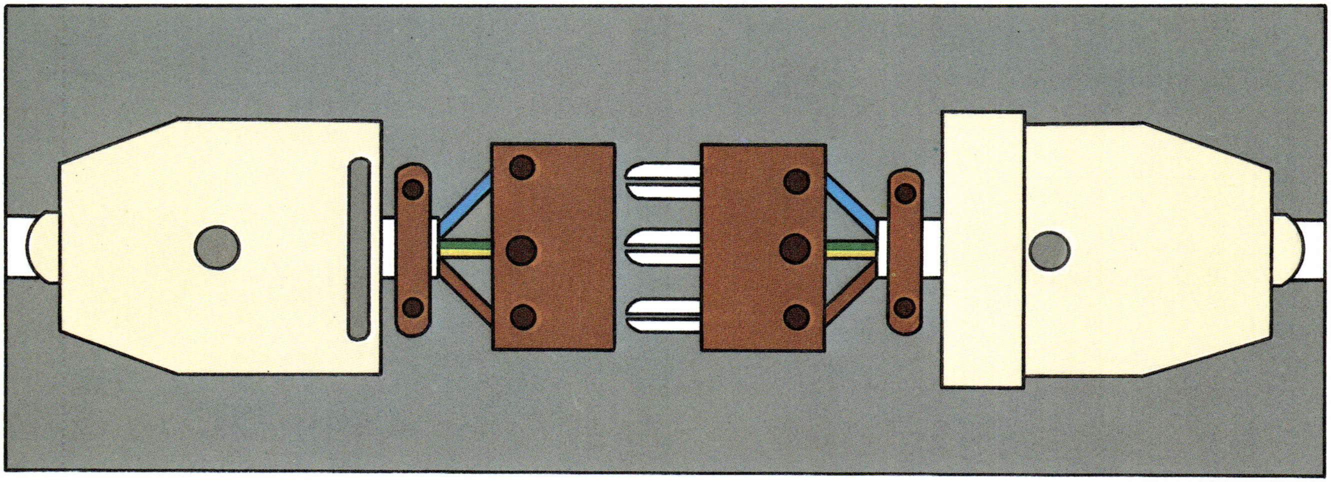

The wiring procedure is the same for detachable connectors, but make sure that the flex from the appliance is connected to the male (pin) half of the connector and the flex to the socket outlet connected to the female (socket) half. And check that live, neutral and earth conductors are paired up on the same terminal and not mixed. Two-pin connectors are available, but these should only be used with double-insulated appliances or those with a low rating, such as a table lamp where earthing is not required.

7 Lights and switches

The lighting circuits in your home will be one of two types. Earlier systems incorporated junction boxes, whereas more recent installations use ceiling roses with built-in terminal blocks. This type of wiring is known as the loop-in method. Both work on the principle of supplying power from the lighting circuits to individual light fittings.

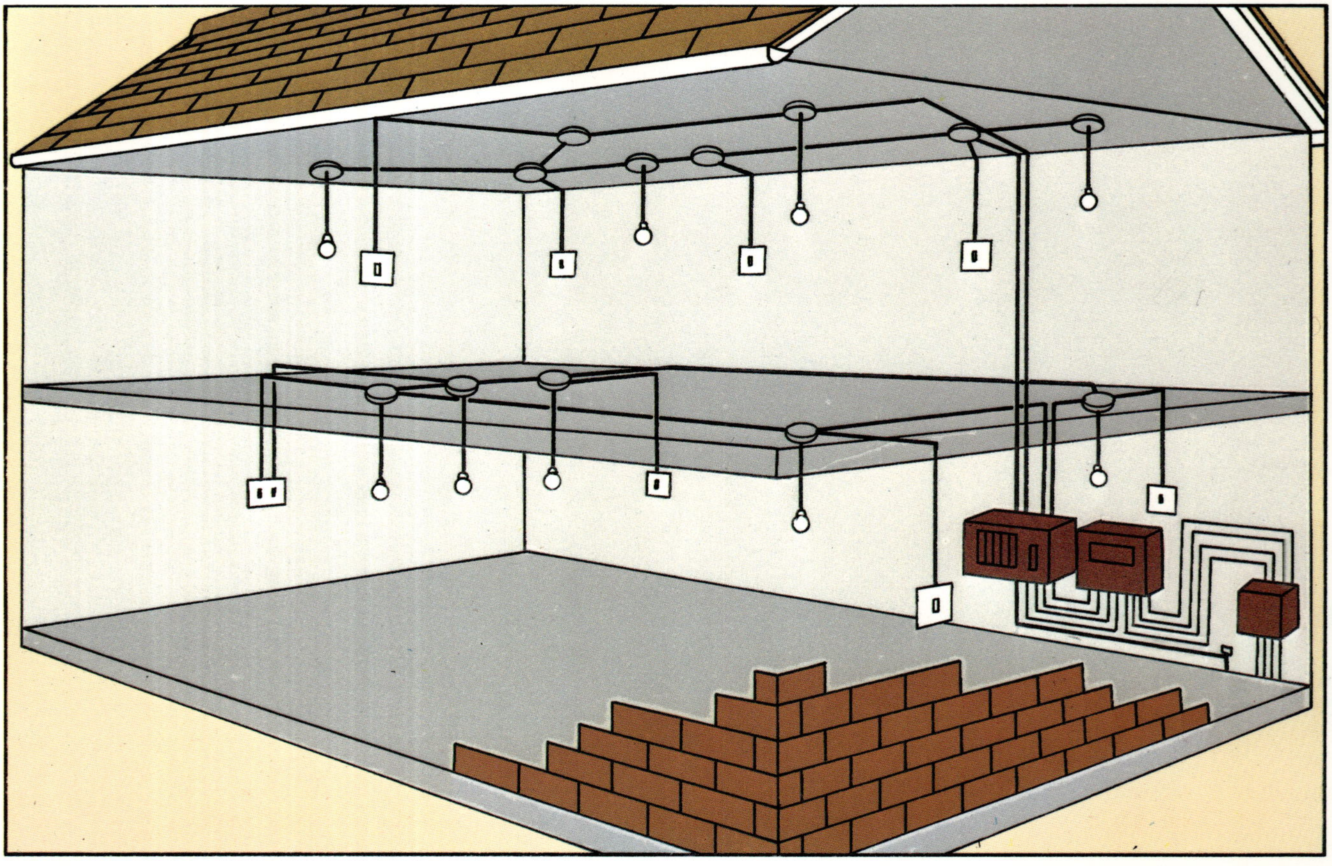

Usually homes will have one lighting circuit for each floor, each circuit having its own 5amp fuse in the consumer unit. This means that a single circuit can carry a total loading of 1kW – the equivalent of ten 100 watt bulbs or any other combination up to 1kW. Check on and familiarise yourself with the system in your home.

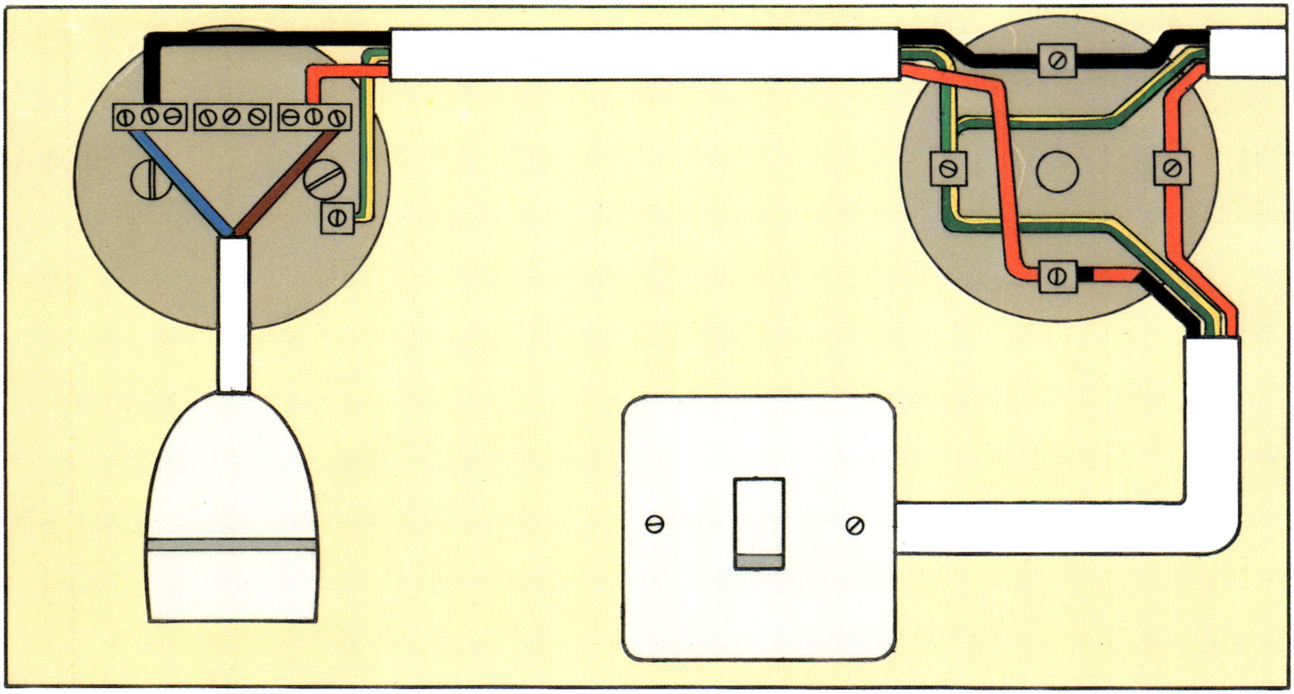

Junction box method

With this method, a lighting circuit is taken from the consumer unit to a junction box, from where the first switch and light-fitting cables radiate. A further cable then runs on to the next junction box and so on around the house. In some older houses the lighting circuit is carried in twin-core cable with no earth conductor. This system is safe enough as long as all the light fittings are made from insulating materials. But problems will arise if a metal pendant is to be fitted – and here a separate earth wire must be installed (see pages 11–12, 21).

The traditional method of wiring in the old-fashioned ceiling rose and light switch was via a junction box, through which the lighting circuit cable ran into the next junction box, which in turn fed another ceiling rose and its switch. Apart from the circuit cable in and out of the box, a third cable fed the ceiling rose and a fourth went to the switch.

Loop-in method

Here the ceiling rose fitting incorporates a terminal block which allows the connection of both the switch cable and the lighting circuit. Provision is also made for earth conductors to be fitted – and this is essential when you want to use a light fitting that requires earthing.

The lighting circuit runs from the consumer unit to the first ceiling fitting, from where the switch cable and light-fitting flex run. The lighting circuit continues to subsequent sets of fittings.

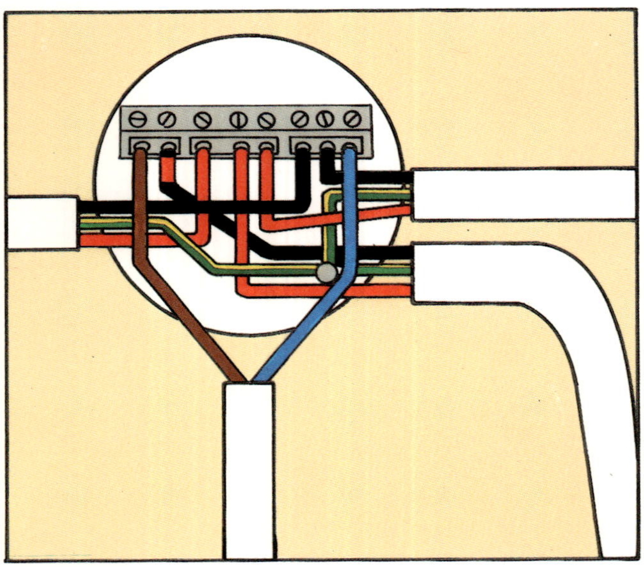

The modern method of wiring in lights dispenses with the junction box. The lighting circuit cable runs directly from one ceiling rose to another. From the terminal block inside the ceiling rose itself a third cable is fed to the light switch and onto this block is also connected the lampholder flex.

Ceiling roses

You will find two types of ceiling rose – the pendant and the batten lampholder. The pendant type is intended for use with a single light bulb (or set of bulbs as in some multiple lamp fittings), which hangs down from the rose. The rose itself is fitted to the ceiling and the lampholder is attached with a length of PVC-covered flex. In older homes you may find this flex is twisted and textile-braided.

Modern types have a terminal block with provision for three live connections (one to the

Traditional pendant light fittings used twisted textile-braided flex. This, however, is liable to damage from overheating, particularly through ageing. Modern fittings use PVC covered flex, which is more durable. If a lampholder is made of metal, it should be earthed and here the flex must be three-core to allow you to do this. Batten lampholders are also available, which allow you to fit a light direct to the wall or ceiling.

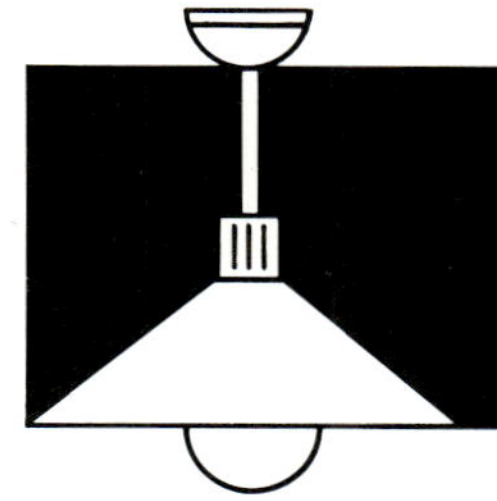

switch, one from the consumer unit and one to the next rose), three neutral connections (one to the lampholder, one from the consumer unit and one to the next rose), two switch connections (one from the switch and one to the lampholder) and also an earth junction terminal.

The batten type is very similar, but it has no hanging flex to a lampholder, since this is fixed onto the fitting.

Both types of rose include a suitable base, which is fitted onto the ceiling by means of screws. Make sure, however, that you have a secure fitting by screwing into either a joist in the ceiling or a suitably positioned piece of timber between two joists (see page 64).

Older roses will not have the loop terminal block and usually require a plastic base or hardwood plinth to enable them to be fixed securely onto the ceiling).

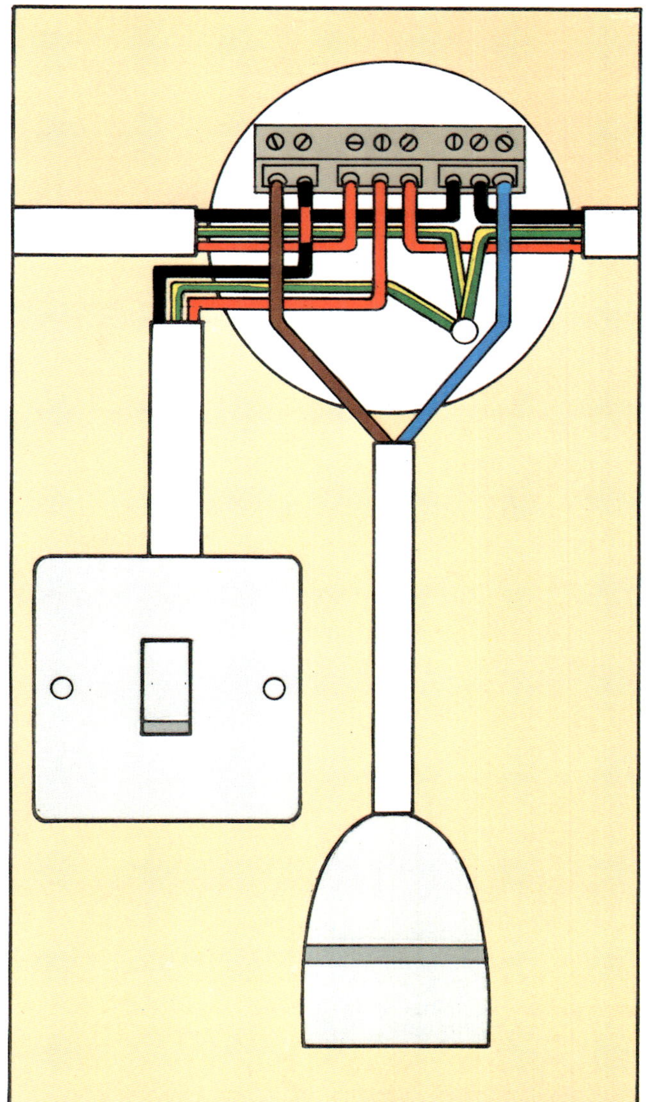

This is the wiring for a typical light fitting. The earth conductors from the three cables – the circuit cables in and out and the switch cable – share a common earth terminal. In this case the lampholder is not metal and therefore does not have an earth conductor. There are three sets of terminals on the terminal block. The right-hand set takes the neutral conductors from the two circuit cables and the lampholder flex. The centre set takes the live conductors from the two circuit cables and the switch cable and the left-hand set takes the live conductor from the lampholder flex and the black (neutral) conductor from the switch cable, which should carry a red sleeve and is 'switched live' – that is, it is live when the switch is on. The last ceiling rose on the circuit will only have one circuit cable fitted – the one going into the rose.

Cut a piece of 100 x 50mm (4 x 2in) timber to fit tightly between adjacent joists. Then drill a 25mm (1in) diameter hole in the desired position in the block. Fix it to the joists at either side by nailing at a 45° angle through the sides of the joists into the new timber block.

Lampholders

These are usually made of plastic and incorporate a simple cord-grip. They only have two terminals for the flex connections – one live and one neutral – and a screwed ring is fitted to the lower half to hold a suitable shade in place. Metal lampholders will have provision for an earth conductor, however.

After long, continual use – particularly with high-wattage bulbs – the lampholders become brittle. You may find the bulb is difficult to replace and the shade ring locks onto the fitting. When this happens, it is time to replace the lampholder (see pages 72–73). You should also inspect the flex in case the insulation has hardened and become brittle or worn. If it has, replace the flex as well (see pages 72–73).

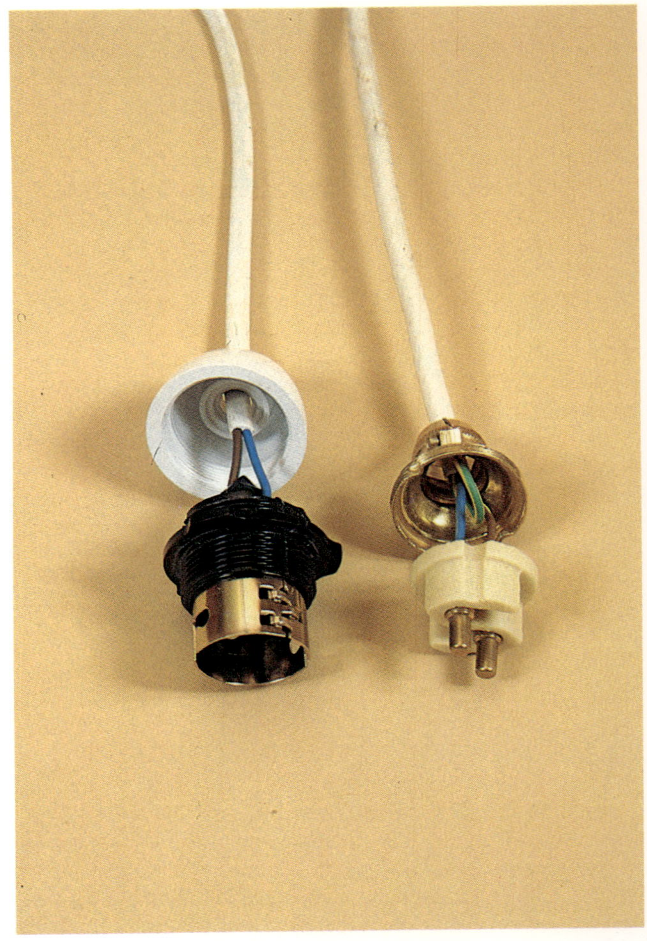

When wiring up a lampholder, it does not matter which of the two terminals are used to connect up the brown and blue conductors of the lampholder flex. But remember that if your lampholder is metal, you must use three-core flex and connect the green/yellow conductor to the earth terminal in the lampholder.

You can get lampholders that are made from brass or other metals – and the obvious advantage here is that they will last indefinitely and not become brittle. But remember, because they are made of metal, they will have to be earthed and this means connecting them to the rose with a three-core flex instead of the normal two-core flex. You will see that there is a special connection on the metal lampholder to which the earth conductor should be fixed in order to earth the metal part of the fitting (see pages 110–111 for fitting techniques).

Lampshades

When you buy a lampshade, always check to see if there is a recommendation on the wattage of bulb to be used with it. Good quality shades are supplied with a small label advising you of the maximum safe wattage of bulb. This should never be exceeded; the consequences could be disastrous, particularly if the shade melts or catches fire.

When you are fixing a shade onto a batten-type lampholder, it is most important you make sure there is a gap between the top of the shade and the ceiling to allow the hot air generated from the bulb to flow away freely and avoid any part of the fitting overheating.

Striplights

There are two types of striplight available – the small incandescent strip and the larger fluorescent tube.

The small striplights are similar to a normal bulb in that the light comes from a white hot element, the difference being that with a strip the element has been straightened out. One connection is fitted to each end of the tube.

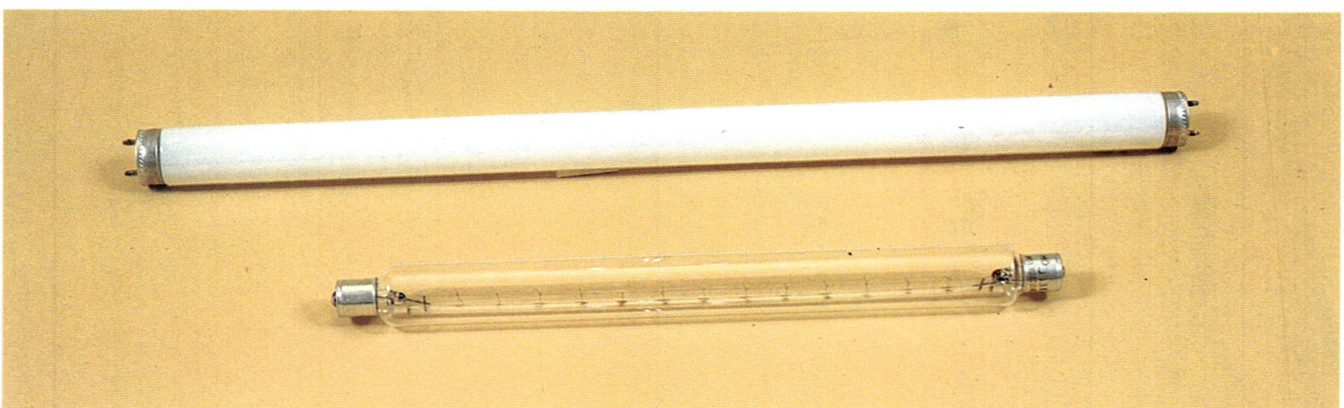

The incandescent striplight is like a normal bulb 'stretched out' and has a contact point at each end of the tube. You can see the incandescent wire running inside the length of the tube. The fluorescent tube works on a different principle. The opaque tube is filled with mercury vapour which 'fluoresces' under certain electrical conditions giving off an intense light. This lamp must be earthed and is fitted into a special holder, which contains a mechanism to activate the light. In some cases this is replaceable.

This type of strip is used, for example, in bedroom vanity units, bathroom units and as internal lighting in such things as cocktail cabinets. The strip is usually of low wattage.

Fluorescent tubes work on a different principle. They are filled with mercury vapour which, under certain circumstances, can be made to conduct electricity. When this happens the vapour fluoresces, giving off an intense white light.

This type of tube is available in many different lengths and colours. The most common are fitted with two pins at each end; these fit into a special holder.

This lighting is more efficient than the traditional bulb since the same amount of light can be obtained from a tube of lower wattage than that from a higher wattage light bulb.

Because the tubes are heavy, they need a strong, secure fixing. They also need to be earthed. And when disposing of them, take good care since you can be cut quite badly if they break. Ideally you should put them in an old bag or wrap them in newspaper before you throw them away.

Switches

With older lighting installations, switches were screwed onto hardwood plinths which were, in turn, screwed onto the wall. Most modern installations, however, use switch plates which are screwed onto a surface or recessed wall-mounting box, through which all the necessary connections are run.

Switches are normally fitted at a standard height of 1370mm (or 4ft 6in) above the floor – and this is an obvious safety precaution if you want to keep them away from young hands. However, in modern houses the light switches are often fitted lower down so that children can operate them. There are many variations of switches available and here are some of the most popular.

One-way switch This type is used where a light is only controlled by one switch – as the name implies.

The old type of light switch was mounted on a wooden plinth (pattress) which was screwed to the wall.

The switch has two connectors at the back of the plate for the cable conductors – one switched live (L2) and one live (common). An earth connection is usually fitted to the wall-mounting box.

Two-way switch This type is used where two or more switches control the same light. It has three connections at the back of the plate, one labelled common (or C) and the others usually L1 and L2. A two-way switch may be used to replace a one-way switch, but never vice-versa.

Variations are available where two or three switches are fitted into one switch plate. These may be used in hallways, on landings, etc. where different lights are switched from the same point.

Modern light switches fit over wall-mounting boxes. These are either recessed into the wall to take a flush-mounted switch plate or surface-mounted, where the switch plate protrudes from the wall. The boxes are fitted onto the wall and the switch plates, with connections on the back, screwed onto them.

A single switch – this can be one-way (the only switch operating a light) or two-way (where the same light is operated by a second switch, which is wired in to the first switch).

Double and triple-gang switches (to enable you to operate two or three lights from the same switchplate). Multiple gang switches are always two-way, with facilities to wire in a second switch to operate each light.

Dimmer switch This device is used to reduce or increase the brilliance of a light to the level required. It is available in various types. The simplest is a knob that switches from off to full brilliance as you turn it. Its main disadvantage is that you have to reset the required brilliance each time the light is switched on. There is a version available that has a separate on/off switch incorporated with a rotating knob, which sets the required brilliance and maintains it until you want to change it.
Touch switch This type of switch is operated simply by touching it – as the name implies. One touch switches on, another touch switches off. One variation of this type incorporates a dimming device; the first touch switches on and operates the dimmer. Depending on how long you keep your finger on it, the light gets brighter. The second touch switches it off.

Replacing switches

Fortunately all modern switch plates are fully interchangeable, which means that you should be able to fix a different type of switch onto the same wall-mounting box, for example when you are

There is a range of dimmer switches available, whose function is to enable you to control the brilliance of a light. The simplest version incorporates a knob that turns from off to full brilliance, although the disadvantage here is that it has to be reset each time you switch on the light. Other switches are available that have a separate on/off control so that the brilliance can be pre-set to the desired level until you want to change it.

The touch switch is particularly useful since it is much safer than a conventional switch should your hands be damp. This makes it suitable, for example, in the kitchen. Some touch switches also incorporate a dimming device, which works on the length of time you leave your finger on the switch. The longer you keep your finger on the switch, the brighter the light gets. With a second touch you can switch off the light.

The difference between a one-way and a two-way switch is that on a two-way switch there are two live terminals (labelled L1 and L2) as well as a common terminal (C). On the one-way switch there is only one live terminal (L2). The one-way switch is wired with the live (red) conductor connected to the common terminal and the switched live (black with red sleeve) conductor connected to the live (L2) terminal. The earth conductor is connected to the earth terminal on the wall-mounting box. With a two-way switch wiring, always use the three-core and earth cable. The switch cable from the light has its live (red) conductor connected to the L1 terminal and the switched live (black with red sleeve) conductor connected to the L2 terminal. The earth conductor is connected to the wall-mounting box. With the cable linking the two switches, the yellow conductor is connected to the L1 terminal in each switch, the blue conductor to the L2 terminal and the red conductor to the common terminal. In each case the earth (bare) conductor with a green/yellow plastic sleeve on it is connected to the wall-mounting box.

changing a normal switch for a dimmer switch or just replacing an old or damaged switch with a new one.

When replacing a switch the very first thing to do is switch off at the main consumer unit. Then you must remove the switch plate, which is attached to the wall-mounting box by two retaining screws. This will enable you to lift the plate away from the wall. The conductors will be attached to the back of this plate, so you will only be able to pull the plate a short distance from the wall.

Check that the connections on the substitute plate are similarly labelled to those on the old plate. Never disconnect before checking the labelling. Loosen the screws and remove the cable conductors from the old switch one by one, making sure you connect each to the equivalent terminals on the new switch. Tighten the screws to secure each connection.

If you are fitting a dimmer switch in place of an ordinary one-way switch, the method of connection

When replacing a switch, before you do any work on the circuit make sure you have switched off at the consumer unit or removed the fuse from that particular lighting circuit. Remove the switch plate by undoing the two retaining screws and lift the plate, with the conductors still attached to the back, from the wall. Make a note of which terminal each conductor is connected to and, if necessary, label each one.

Loosen each terminal screw in turn and remove the conductor. If the wiring has not been looked at for some time, the conductors may need a little persuasion and a pair of pliers could be needed to free them. But don't pull too hard or you will put undue strain on the conductors.

Before you connect up to the new switch, check that the end of each conductor is in good condition – not frayed and with no loose whiskers. Twist the ends as needed or cut off the exposed conductor and strip back a new end (see pages 51-53).

Loosen the terminal screws on the new switch plate and check the layout, since the terminals may not be in exactly the same position as on the old switch plate. Insert the conductors, one by one, into the correct terminals and secure the connections by tightening each screw.

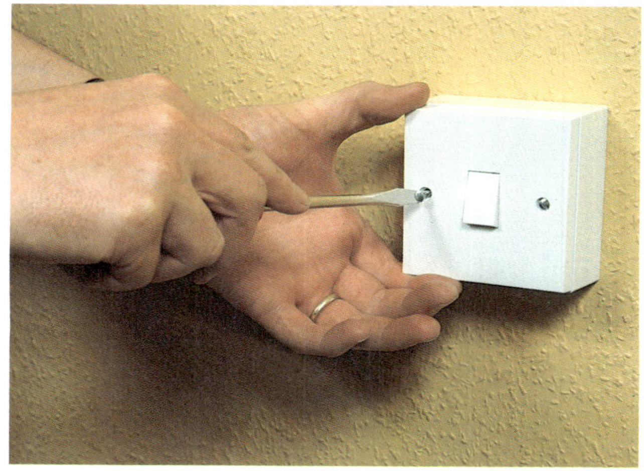

Check all the connections are sound and that the conductors will fit neatly inside the wall-mounting box before you fix on the new switch plate and tighten the retaining screws. Make sure the conductors are not trapped when tightening the screws.

If you find, after wiring up, that the switch works the wrong way – that is, up for off – you may be able to rectify this by turning the switch plate upside down. This will depend on whether the switch looks the same either way up and if there is enough slack in the cable so that you do not twist or overstretch the conductors. If not, you should be able to solve the problem by moving the black conductor onto the spare L terminal. Don't move the red conductor, which is connected to the common terminal.

will be similar, although the terminals may be in a slightly different position on the back of the plate. Make sure you connect the red conductor to the terminal marked common (or C) and the black conductor to the L2 terminal.

Check that the connections have been made to the right terminals and that the screws are tightened to ensure a firm grip on the conductors. Before you fix the plate back on the wall-mounting box, make sure none of the conductors are twisted or liable to be trapped when the plate is re-fixed. Fix on the new switch plate by tightening the two retaining screws.

Turn on at the mains and try the switch. If you have replaced a one-way switch with a two-way switch, you may find that the switch works the wrong way – that is, up for on. If this happens, you can remedy the problem in one of two ways.

Switch off at the mains, remove the retaining screws and lift the plate clear. You may be able to rotate the plate 180 degrees, provided none of the wires at the back are twisted or will be trapped when the plate is replaced.

If this does not prove possible – or if the switch is so designed only to be fitted one way up – you should be able to solve the problem by moving the black conductor onto the spare L terminal. Don't move the red conductor that is connected to the common terminal.

Replacing a plastic lampholder and flex

The plastic lampholder tends to become brittle in use and will need replacing from time to time. Overheating may also affect the flex connecting the lampholder to the ceiling rose, causing the insulation to become brittle and therefore dangerous. But both are quite easily replaced.

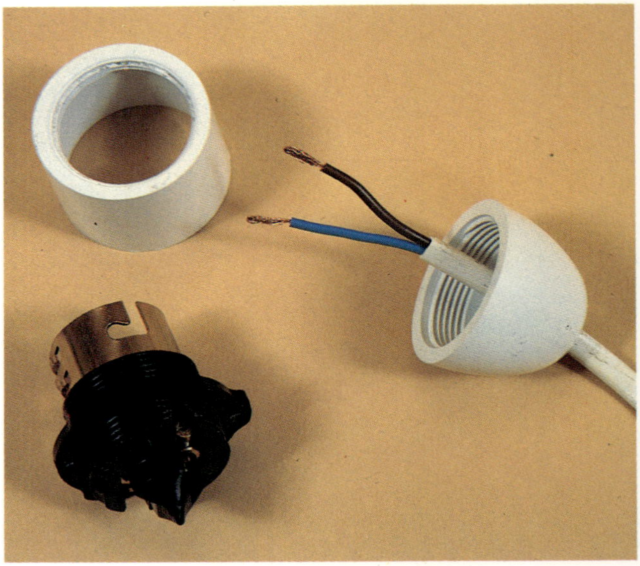

If you need to change a lampholder and flex on a pendant light fitting, first prepare the new length of flex, removing about 25mm (1in) of the outer insulation and about 15mm (5/8in) of the conductor insulation at each end. Twist the exposed end of each conductor and double it over. Unscrew the cover of the new lampholder to expose the terminals.

Connect the blue and brown conductors at one end of the flex to the two terminals on the new lampholder. It does not matter which way round they go. Check that there is no exposed conductor on either side of the terminals and that the connections are secure, then slide the lampholder cover down from the free end of the flex and screw it on.

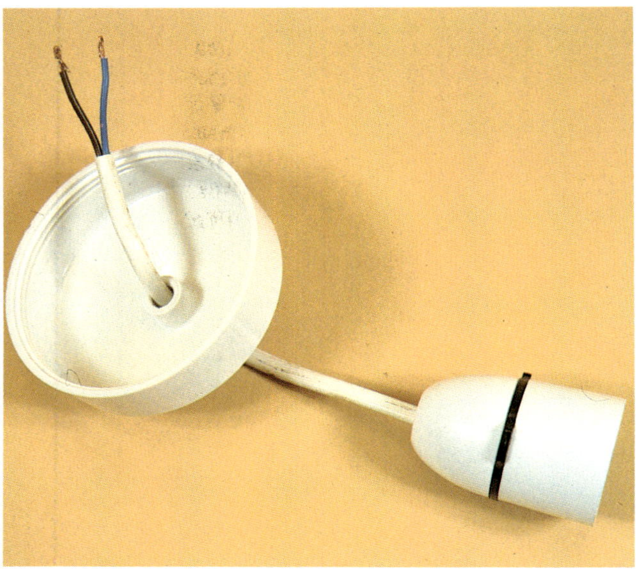

Cut a new length of flex to the required length. Make sure you use 0.5sq mm round flex with PVC sheathing. Remember that with plastic lampholders only a two-core flex is required. Cut back the outer insulation about 25mm (1in) and strip back the conductor insulation about 15mm (⅝in).

Remove the top cover from the new lampholder and connect the brown and blue conductors to the terminals (it does not matter which way round). Slide the lampholder cover over the free end of flex and screw it back in place.

The final connection is to the ceiling rose and, at this stage, you must switch off at the mains. Unscrew the ceiling rose cover and disconnect the old flex. Before making the new connections, don't forget to slip the ceiling rose cover over the new flex. When you have connected up the new flex, replace the rose cover.

Take the bulb and old shade off the original lampholder and refix them on the new one. You may find that you cannot unscrew the holder to free the lampshade, in which case you will have to break the plastic to get the shade off.

You are now ready to make the connections to the ceiling rose. But before you do, make sure you have switched off at the consumer unit or removed the fuse from the relevant lighting circuit. Unscrew the ceiling rose cover and disconnect the old flex. Then slide the cover over the new length of flex.

When wiring up the free end of the lampholder flex, check carefully that the blue conductor is connected to the right-hand set of terminals together with the neutral conductors from the two lighting circuit cables and that the brown conductor is connected to the left-hand set of terminals with the switched live conductor from the switch cable. Ensure the connections are neat and secure, then screw back on the ceiling rose cover. You can now restore the power to that circuit.

8 Power sockets

The power circuit

Older houses fitted with 5amp and 15amp round-pin power socket outlets are wired radially, that is with a separate cable to each socket outlet from the consumer unit. This system is now out of date and if you have it in your home, get it checked by a competent electrician to ensure it is still safe.

Modern installations rely on a ring main circuit, which means that a twin-core and earth 2.5sq mm cable is run from the consumer unit to the first socket outlet. From there a similar cable connects the first socket outlet to the second and so on until the last socket outlet in that particular circuit is reached. Here the cable returns to the consumer unit, thus completing the ring.

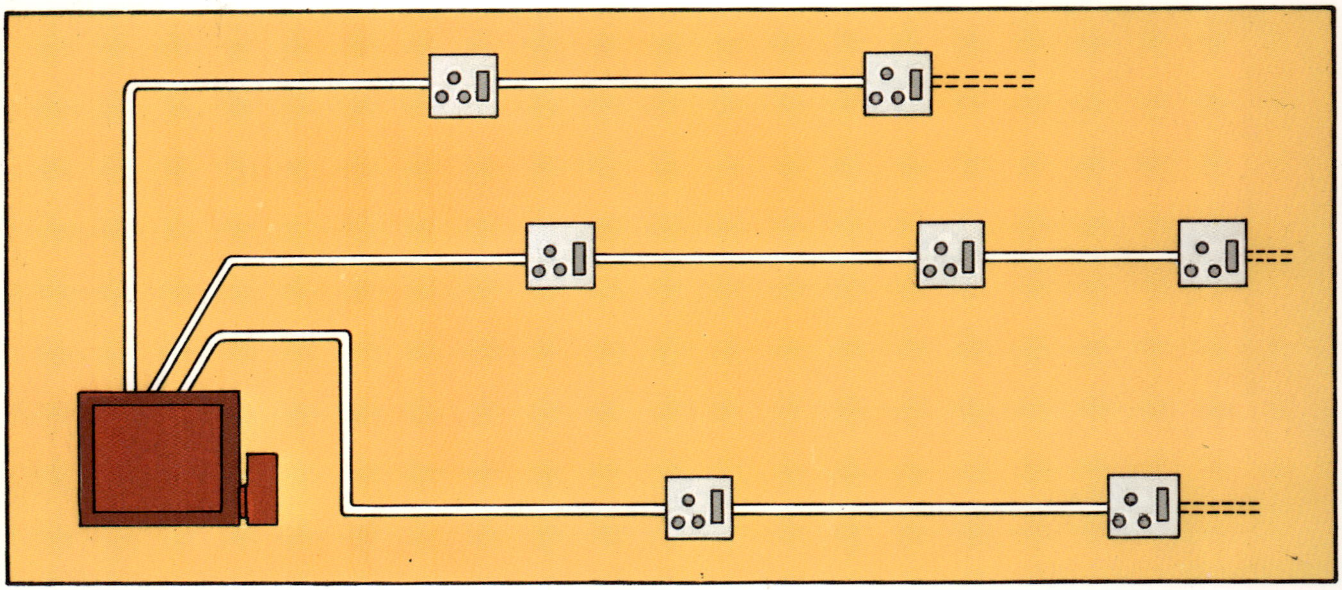

The old system of wiring up the power socket outlets radially is now out of date, and if your home still has this type of circuit you should have it inspected since age may well have rendered it unsafe. With this system a number of socket outlets were fed from one circuit – and there were many circuits radiating out from the consumer unit, each carrying its own 15amp fuse. Original radial circuit wiring is distinguishable by the existence of round-pin sockets and plugs. Another indication is the type of cable used. This could have been single-core running in a steel conduit or lead or rubber covered two or three-core cable. You can check in the loft space to see what type of cable you have in your home, since this is the one area where you can see exposed cables between the joists.

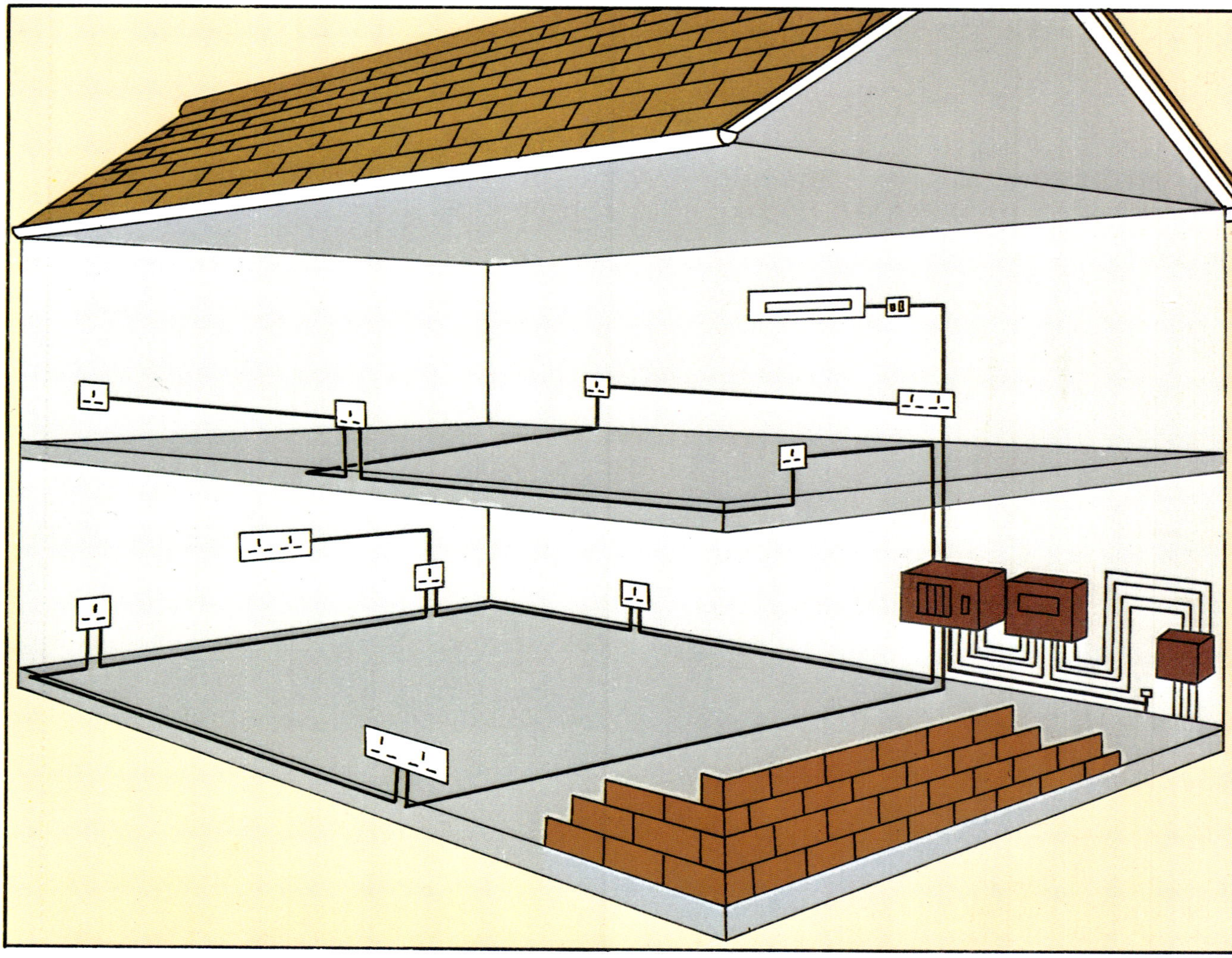

The modern system for wiring incorporates a ring circuit, which links the various power outlets before returning to the consumer unit. Normally each floor of the home will have its own power circuit – and hence 30amp fuse in the consumer unit. Check on and familiarise yourself with the system in your home.

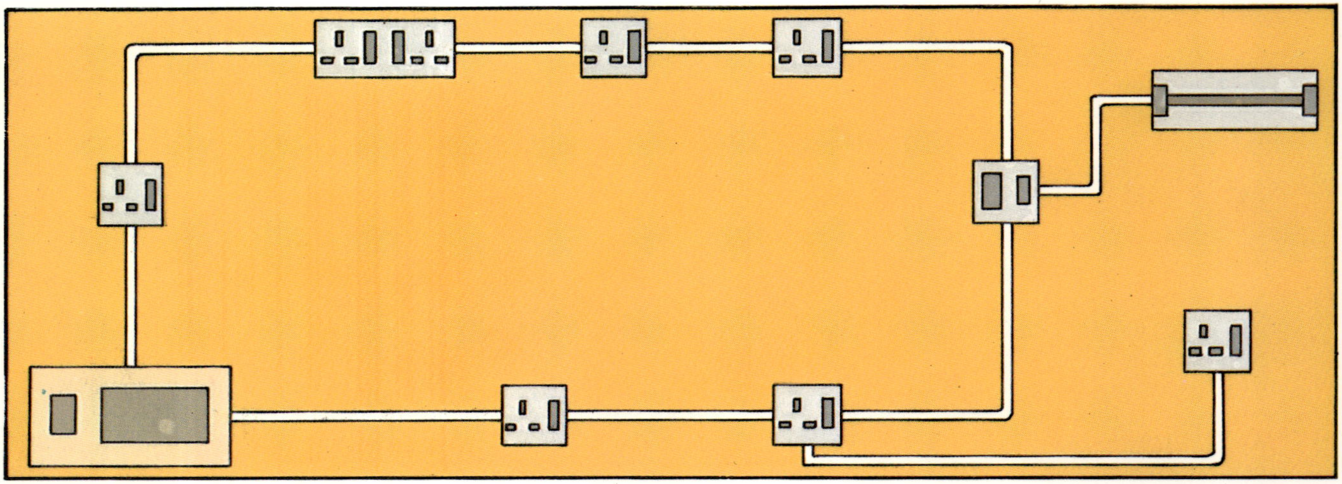

On a ring circuit the cable runs from the consumer unit to the first socket outlet, then on to the next and so on until the last socket outlet, from where the cable is fed back to the consumer unit. This circuit may well incorporate a fused connection unit supplying, for example, a bathroom wall heater. Any socket outlet on a spur (or branch) from the main circuit was almost certainly added after the original installation.

A spur is an extra socket that has been added to the existing circuit and wired into a socket outlet on the ring main circuit that is not already a spur or does not have a spur already fed from it. (To check which socket outlet can be used safely to feed off a spur, see pages 104-105.)

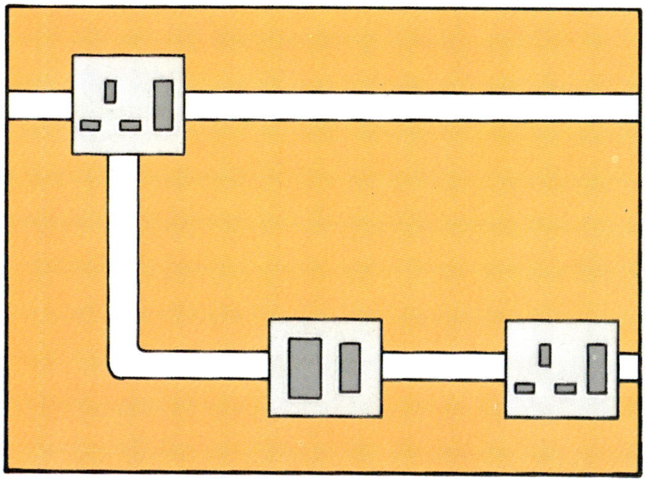

To give added protection to the spur you can fit a fused connection unit on the cable running from the socket outlet on the ring main to the spur socket outlet. This unit can be used with the relevant fuse to limit the load applied to the spur – for example, to prevent an electric fire being plugged in to a socket in a child's bedroom.

It is inevitable that at some time you will feel the need for additional socket outlets. These can be fitted from any ring main outlet except one that is already fed off the main circuit. These additions to a circuit are known as spurs. Only one 13amp socket outlet can be fitted on any one spur, but this outlet could be a twin socket. The total number of fused spurs is unlimited, but the number of non-fused spurs must not exceed the total number of socket outlets and items of stationary equipment connected directly to the circuit.

A spur may also be used to supply one unswitched fused connection unit (see pages 104–109) feeding a permanent fitting such as a bathroom radiant heater.

Socket outlets

Modern socket outlets are plate-mounted, which means that they will fit onto a flush or wall-mounted

As with light switches, socket outlets are available either flush or wall-mounted. Single or double sockets can be installed, the latter being particularly useful where more than one appliance may be used at any one time – such as in the kitchen, or a living room where you might want to use the TV or hi-fi and a lamp. You can get unswitched socket outlets, but the use of these is to be discouraged for safety reasons. If you do have them fitted, make sure you use insulated-pin plugs with them.

box. Most are fitted with a switch (or switches) although they are available without. It is always safer to install a switched socket outlet, otherwise you must remember always to remove the plug from the socket when it is not in use.

On a ring main circuit, any socket outlet will have two sets of conductors connected to each terminal – two to the live terminal, two to the neutral terminal and two to the earth terminal (three if there is a metal wall-mounting box, which requires an earth connection). In a socket outlet from which a spur has been taken, there will be the three sets, the third set feeding the spur. (Remember, all spurs should be wired with the same size cable as the circuits.) The only socket outlets with one set of conductors will be either a single spur outlet or the second spur outlet. One single or one twin-socket outlet is allowed on one spur.

Twin socket outlets are useful where you are

If you want to replace a socket outlet, either because it is damaged or because you want to fit a switched version in place of the existing unswitched outlet, first turn off the power at the consumer unit or remove the fuse from the relevant circuit. Remove the switch plate by undoing the retaining screws and lift it, with the conductors attached, clear of the wall.

Normally there will be two connectors of the same colour going to each terminal, since a socket outlet on the ring main will have a cable going in to the socket and a cable feeding out from it to the next socket. If there is only one set of conductors, then the socket is on a spur. Make a note of where each pair of conductors goes and mark them if necessary. Then release the conductors.

permanently running two appliances nearby – or where one appliance is permanently plugged and you need a spare outlet for a vacuum cleaner, for example.

And remember that you should never wire more than one appliance into a single plug for fear of overloading: this is a dangerous practice, since there is only one fuse for two appliances.

If you decide to change a single outlet into a double, the work is simplified by the fact that no additional connection cables are needed. The socket can be wired in from the existing cables (see pages 80–83).

Replacing a socket outlet

This job is necessary if the switch in the socket outlet breaks down or if you want to change an unswitched outlet into a switched one.

Turn off the power at the mains and check the

Inspect the ends of each conductor to make sure there is no damage. If there is, cut off the end and trim back the cable as you would when preparing a length of flex (see pages 51–53). Then connect the pairs of conductors to their relevant terminals – red to live, black to neutral and green/yellow to earth. Tighten the terminal screws and check the connections are secure.

Before you replace the switch plate, make sure the conductors lie easily inside the socket and will not be pinched or twisted when the switch plate is screwed back on. Finally refix the switch plate onto the wall-mounting box. Check the new outlet is functioning correctly. Restore the power and either plug in an appliance or a special test plug to do this.

circuit is not live with a test meter. Undo the retaining screws that hold the switch plate in position and lift the plate clear from the wall. You will see a set of conductors connected to their relevant terminals on the back of the plate. Free the conductors from their terminals by loosening the screws and re-connect them to the equivalent terminals on the back of the new switch plate – red wires to the live terminal, black wires to the neutral terminal and the green/yellow or bare wires to the earth terminal. Tighten all the terminal screws and make a final check that the right wires are connected to the right terminals.

Before you screw the new switch plate back on, make sure none of the wires are twisted or trapped behind the switch plate. Replace the switch plate by inserting and tightening the retaining screws on the front.

Fitting a double socket outlet in place of a single

No extra wiring is needed when you replace a single socket outlet with a double one. Before you start work, turn off the power at the mains. Then release the retaining screws in the front of the socket plate and lift the plate clear of the wall.

Surface-mounted socket

If the socket outlet is surface-mounted, you will have to remove the wall-mounting box and replace it with a double version. Knock out with the blade of an old chisel the cable-entry holes in the new box and file off any sharp edges. Undo the conductors from their terminals, making a note which one is which (this can be done by wrapping a piece of sticky tape round each conductor and labelling it). Then unscrew the wall-mounting box and take it out.

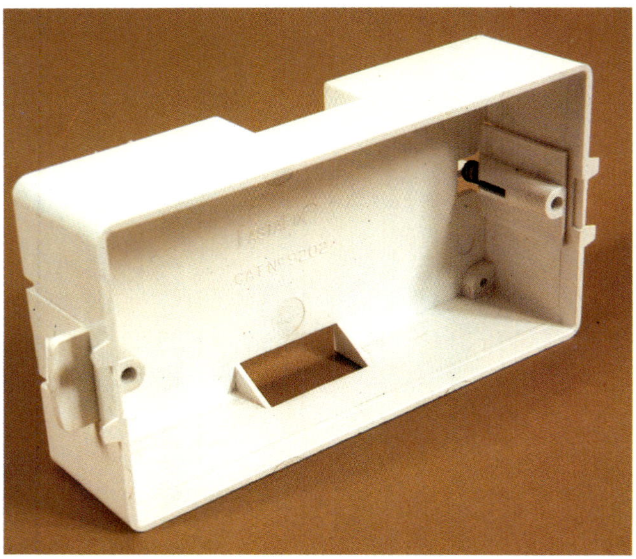

There is a range of wall-mounting boxes to suit all situations and basically they are available for either recessed or surface-mounted fitting. For the recessed boxes you have to make a hole in the wall deep enough to take all the box. Although a shallow version is available, this is rarely used with the normal socket outlet – only the unswitched type. The cable is fed into the box through holes in the side or back, which you must knock out and fit with a rubber grommet to prevent the cable fraying against the bare metal. Surface-mounted boxes made of plastic are screwed onto the wall – and here the cable-entry holes are always in the back of the box. The standard wall boxes provide few problems when fitted to a solid wall. But you will need a specially designed box for fitting to a partition wall. This has lugs on the side which grip the back of the plasterboard skin when the switch plate retaining screws are tightened.

1

2

3

4

5

6

1. If you want to change a single surface-mounted socket outlet for a double one, first switch off the power at the consumer unit or remove the fuse from the relevant circuit. Take off the switch plate by undoing the retaining screws and, having checked how the conductors are wired and labelling them if necessary, disconnect all the conductors. Remove the old wall-mounting box by undoing the fixing screws and lift it from the wall. With the blade of an old chisel, knock out the cable-entry holes in the back of the new box, file down any sharp cut edges and fit grommets in these holes.

2. Then position your new box on the wall, feeding the exposed cable through the knocked-out holes in the back of the box.

3. Trace the outline of the new box on the wall with a pencil, marking where the screws will go through the fixing holes already drilled in the back of the box. Lift the box clear and check that these holes do not clash with the cable runs either side of the box. If they do, you will have to adjust the position of the box fractionally so that the fixing screws miss the two cables. Normally cable runs vertically. Before you finalise the position, check that the conductors are long enough to reach the switch plate when you need to make the connections. Drill the holes to take the screws and plug them.

4. Feed the two ends of cable back through the cable-entry holes and screw the wall-mounting box in position.

5. Connect up the two sets of conductors, making sure you match red with red and connect these to the live terminal, black with black to the neutral terminal and green/yellows to the earth terminal. Check that the connections are secure

6. Before you screw on the new switch plate, make sure the conductors inside lie neatly and will not be twisted or pinched when the switch plate is in position. Finally fix on the new switch plate and restore the power to the circuit.

Feed the conductors through the knock-out holes in the new box and position the box on the wall. Mark with a pencil through the fixing holes and then lift the box clear. Check to ensure that the fixing positions do not clash with the existing cable runs. If they do, you will have to move the box fractionally. There should be enough slack in the cables to allow a slight adjustment. If there isn't, you will have to move the box further along the cable.

When you have worked out the best position for the box and marked the fixing points on the wall, drill two holes with a No. 8 masonry drill bit (if the wall is made of brick or building blocks). Insert wall plugs into the two holes and fix the box in position with the fixing screws. (If you are working on a partition wall, see pages 102–103).

Following carefully the correct order for wiring – red to live, black to neutral and green/yellow or bare to earth – fix the three conductors to their relevant terminals on the back of the new switch plate. Checking that the right connections have been made and that the wires are not twisted or trapped, fix the new double socket plate onto the box with the retaining screws.

Using an electric drill

When installing certain electrical fittings, you may find it necessary to use an electric drill – for example, to drill holes in the wall to take the wall-mounting box. And it may well be that you have reached that stage in the installation where you must switch off the power in order to work safely on the existing wiring.

The solution is to isolate the circuit on which you are working, but keep another power circuit – which will normally be on another floor – switched on so that you can plug in your electric drill. Of course, you will need plenty of extension cable to run between the floors to the area in which you are working.

Switch off at the mains and then locate the fuse in the circuit you want to isolate. If your fuses are not labelled, you will have to identify the relevant fuse by trial and error. You can usefully use the opportunity to label them. Take out each fuse in turn and plug a lamp into the socket you are working on. If it does not work – and there are no faults – then the circuit feeding that socket outlet is dead and you can work on it in safety, while allowing the power to run through the other circuits in the home.

The alternative to this is, of course, to use a hand drill, although this will be much harder work, particularly when you are drilling into brickwork.

Flush-mounted socket

If the outlet you want to replace is flush-mounted, there are two possible methods. The first depends on whether there is enough spare cable in the wall-mounting box to enable you to fix a slim surface-mounted box in front of the existing recessed one.

If there is enough cable to feed forward, you can fix a surface-mounted box as described above. If there is not enough slack in the cable to do this, you will have to remove the existing box and fit in a new double box (see pages 85–88).

When you take out the old box, a certain amount of plaster is bound to come away from the edge of the hole. This won't matter since you are going to enlarge the hole anyway. Hold the new double box in position on the wall and mark its position all round the edges with a pencil.

One useful tip to avoid excessive damage to the surrounding plaster is to score the marked perimeter of the wall-mounting box with a sharp knife before drilling.

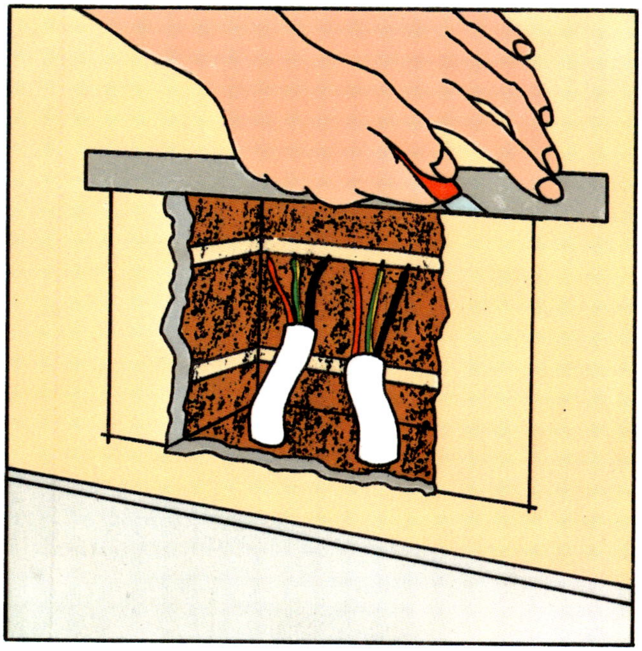

If you want to fit a flush-mounted double socket outlet, you may find you have to remove the existing single wall-mounting box and fit in a double one. This will involve making a larger hole in the wall to take the new box. First switch off the power at the consumer unit or remove the fuse from the relevant circuit. Remove and disconnect the existing switch plate, checking where each conductor goes and labelling if necessary. You will have to remove the old wall-mounting box, which may be firmly wedged in the wall even after you have removed the fixing screws. In this case chip away with a club hammer and cold chisel to remove the surrounding plaster. It will not matter how much damage you do either side of the box since you will be enlargening the opening afterwards. Pull the old box clear with a pair of pliers gripping one edge.

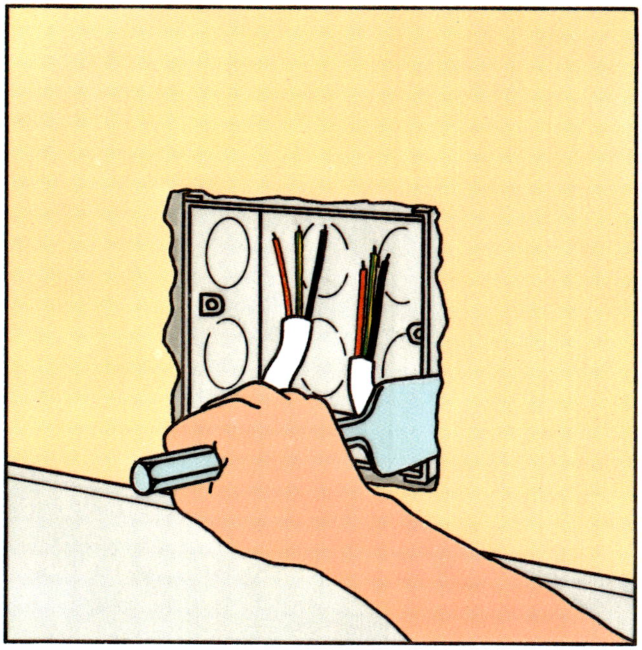

Before you start opening up the hole, check where the cable runs are and mark these clearly on the wall to make sure you do not damage them while you work. Extend the marks beyond the position of the new double socket so that you do not drill into them when screwing down the new box should the cable run horizontally. Hold the new box in position on the wall and, when you are satisfied that its fixing will not interfere with the cables, mark the outline in pencil. Then chip a groove carefully around the perimeter. This will help stop the plaster cracking around the hole as you clear it out.

Measure the depth of the new wall-mounting box and mark this distance with a piece of sticky tape on the drill bit. This will ensure you drill to the correct depth for the box, since you stop drilling when the sticky tape reaches the wall surface. Drill a series of holes just inside the perimeter groove you have already chipped out. This will make the chiselling away of the brickwork that much easier.

Chisel away the brickwork with a brick bolster and club hammer to the depth of the drilled holes and, as you get near to the edges, check whether the box will fit the new opening. It should lie just below the wall surface. You do not want to chip away more than you need, in order to keep the amount of replastering round the new opening to a minimum when the box is installed.

A word of warning. When you take out the old box, you will see in which direction the cables run. Mark this clearly so that you don't accidentally drill into these areas – and therefore into the existing cable. Generally cable runs vertically, not horizontally.

When you have drilled round the perimeter of the proposed new hole, chip away the plaster and brickwork with a club hammer and cold chisel. When you get near to the edge of the marked area, keep testing with the new box until it slots tightly into the new hole. This will save you extra work repairing the surrounding plaster when the new box is fitted.

You may have to knock out holes in each side of the new box to take the cable into and out of the box. When you have knocked out the relevant holes, fit grommets into each; this will prevent the cable from rubbing against the sharp edges of the holes and chafing. When you come to test the box in

When the opening is the correct size, clean out the debris. Knock out holes in the new wall-mounting box to take the cables and fit grommets in them. Then feed in the two ends of cable and position the box in the wall. Mark off where the fixing holes come, remove the box and drill and plug these holes ready to take the fixing screws when the box is in position.

Feed the cable ends back through the box and screw the box into the new opening. Make sure your cable is fully stretched and will not be pinched or twisted as the box is screwed into place. Arrange the three conductors in the new wall-mounting box so that each conductor corresponds with its position on the switch plate ready for connection. Check the ends of the conductors are not damaged.

the hole, you must first feed the lengths of cable through these knock-out holes. When you slide the box in, take great care that the cables do not get caught in between the sides of the box and the wall.

Make sure, when you chip out the new hole, that the back of the hole is as flat and smooth as possible. Ideally when the hole is completed the new box should be about 3mm (⅛in) in from the wall surface. When you are satisfied the hole is the right size to accept the new double box, clean out all the debris from the hole.

At the back of the box there will be two fixing holes. Insert the box and mark these positions on the wall. Take the box out, drill the holes and insert wall plugs ready to take the box retaining screws.

Insert the box and fix it to the wall with the retaining screws. Before you connect up the cables to the switch plate of the double socket, make good the damaged area around the new box with a plaster filler.

Before you fix on the switch plate, make good the damaged area around the wall-mounting box with plaster filler. Spread this on carefully with a filling knife, making sure you do not get any plaster inside the box. Try to get as smooth a finish on the plaster as you can by going over the surface with the filling knife wetted. If necessary you can always rub down the plaster with medium glasspaper when it has dried.

When you have completed the repair work to the wall, make the necessary connections – red conductors to the live terminal, black conductors to the neutral terminal and green/yellow conductors to the earth terminal – and screw the switch plate onto the new box. Remember you will need an extra piece of green/yellow conductor from the E terminal on the switch plate to that on a metal wall-mounting box.

With the box firmly in place and the area around it made good, you can now connect up the conductors from each cable to their relevant terminals on the switch plate – red to live, black to neutral and green/yellow or bare to earth. Make sure that you connect a short length of conductor covered with a green/yellow sleeve between the E terminal in the socket plate and that in the box.

Finally make sure that the new outlets are functioning correctly. Restore the power to the circuit and either plug in an appliance or use a test plug.

The last stage is to check the correct connections have been made and that the wires are not twisted or trapped before you fix the switch plate onto the box with the retaining screws provided.

Fused connection units provide extra protection to either lighting or power circuits if wired in between the source of supply and the fitting or appliance. They are available for either flush or surface-mounted fitting and can either be switched or unswitched – sometimes incorporating an indicator light to show when the power is switched on. You can use them to convert from a cable to a flex – to feed a wall-mounted heater, for example – or to run a light off the power circuit, in which case the unit is fitted with a 3amp fuse.

Fused connection unit

This unit provides extra protection in either a lighting or power circuit. Like a socket outlet, it can be flush or surface-mounted. It can be a means of converting from a cable to a flex and one obvious example of this function is in a bathroom, where the unit feeds the supply to a wall-mounted heater, which is connected to the unit by means of a flex.

The unit can be either switched or unswitched and is sometimes fitted with an indicator light to show when the supply is switched on.

Another example of its use is for an outside light, which may be wired through the fused connection unit to the power circuit. Although the power circuit carries a 30amp fuse, by fitting a 3amp fuse in the unit you can convert safely to supply power for the light. It is wired into a circuit in a similar way to a socket outlet and carries an additional fuse. (For wiring in a fused connection unit, see pages 108–109).

9 Adding to the circuit

With a new house, the builder – or possibly even the buyer – decides where all the various electrical fittings – lights, switches, socket outlets – should go to ensure the most convenience and ease of use. Inevitably, however, as family circumstances change, the need arises for additional fittings. These might include extra socket outlets, new fittings for wall lights, extra switches for existing lights or even a switched fused connection unit to supply a bathroom heater.

With the experience gained in doing basic electrical jobs in the home – and by following the instructions given here – these tasks are well within the scope of the competent DIY worker. But remember the safety rules at all times and, if in doubt, check with a qualified electrician before you start any work on the circuit and make sure you test it carefully on completion of the job.

When adding any electrical fitting to existing circuits – whatever the situation is – there are certain basic jobs you will have to undertake.

Running cable

Before you commit yourself to positioning your new electrical fitting, check to see where the cable has to run to and, if necessary, draw a small plan to work out the ideal route.

As a general rule, fix light switches about 1370mm (4ft 6in) above the floor and power socket outlets at least 150mm (6in) above the floor or work surface. Of course you can vary the position to suit your own needs. For example, if you find difficulty bending down to plug in appliances and switch them on and off, you may find it more convenient to fit power socket outlets higher up the wall within easier reach. But remember electrical fittings should never be positioned less than 150mm (6in) from the

There are many different ways of running cable through the home – and each time you are faced with this job you will have to weigh up the pros and cons and decide on merit. Suffice it to say that the shortest route from A to B may be the cheapest but is rarely practical. One important point to bear in mind is that cable should always be run vertically where possible, as a safety precaution. This makes tracing it later that much easier and will help anyone working near it to avoid it.

floor to avoid mechanical damage from, for example, a vacuum cleaner or children's toys.

Bear in mind that a minor adjustment to the position of the fitting may make the job a lot easier.

The shortest distance between the two ends of cable will work out the cheapest, but remember that it is still important that the cable runs vertically, especially if it is to be buried in plaster where it will be hidden. The reason for this is quite simple. It gives anyone working in the area later a reasonable chance of locating the cable run and not damaging the wiring – or getting a shock from hitting or touching a live conductor.

One point to bear in mind if you are recessing cable in plaster is that you should not tamper with fresh decorations – particularly new plaster. It is better to leave your cable exposed for a few weeks to allow any new decoration to settle before channelling it in.

There are several methods you can use to run cable to your new fitting. These include any of the following:

1. In roof spaces along and through joists.
2. Beneath floorboards.
3. Along and through rafters above ceilings.
4. Below suspended floors resting on a concrete sub-floor.
5. Down cavity and partition walls (see pages 97–98, 102–103).
6. On the surface of walls and ceilings.
7. Buried in plaster.
8. Through conduits.
9. Along special skirting board trunking.

NOTE Never run cable under floor coverings or along the bottom of skirting boards where it could easily be damaged either by a vacuum cleaner or by excessive traffic in that area.

Embedding cable in plaster

Having decided on the ideal route for the new cable, mark with a pencil and straight-edge where it will run on the wall. Make sure you run the cable vertically. The accepted rule is never to work immediately above or below an electrical fitting, So by keeping to the rule you will make your life – and other people's – a great deal easier.

Having marked the route for the cable, you will now have to channel out the plaster to take the cable. Make sure this is deep enough for the cable to lie at least 6mm (¼in) below the surface of the wall to allow a reasonable covering of plaster on top.

You can either make this channel with a bolster chisel and club hammer or use a plaster router attachment on an electric drill.

First score the marked lines with a cutting knife. This will help prevent the surrounding plaster from flaking or cracking as you work round the hole. It is also a good idea to drill a series of holes with a masonry drill along the line of the cable to avoid damage to the surrounding plaster.

If you use a router, you would be well advised to pin a strip of batten along one edge of the proposed cable run to act as a guide and help ensure that you cut the channel straight.

Depending on the thickness of the plaster, you may have to channel into some of the brickwork as well. Here again, the brickwork will chip away more easily if you drill a series of holes into the brick first. Usually the cable should lie comfortably within the normal thickness of plaster.

When turning corners in the channel, make sure you arc the bend, so that the cable runs smoothly round the corner and does not catch on any sharp edge. Lay the cable in the channel and check that it lies at least 6mm (¼in) below the surface. If not, you will have to channel out more until it does.

Smear contact adhesive at regular intervals

When running cable in plaster, first check where other cable runs might be by looking at nearby fittings and avoiding working in a line immediately above or below them. Take care too that your route does not cross an existing cable run. These considerations are relevant in deciding the final position of your new fitting. Once established, mark its position in pencil on the wall and, with a straight-edge, draw two parallel lines from the fitting. The lines should be wide enough apart to take the cable you are using. Normally the depth of plaster is sufficient for burying the cable. If it is less than 12mm (½in) thick, however, you will have to remove some of the brickwork as well. Chip away carefully between the marked lines to remove the plaster – and, if necessary, some of the brickwork – testing the depth by inserting the cables as you work. If you score the marked lines with a sharp knife before you chip away with the cold chisel and club hammer, you will restrict the damage to the plaster either side of the channel. When your run is complete, insert the cable. It will help if you put a little contact adhesive on the back of the cable at intervals to hold it in place while you cover over the run with a quick-drying plaster filler. Apply the finishing plaster as smoothly as possible to minimise the rubbing down afterwards.

A quicker and less arduous method of cutting out a channel is with a router attachment to an electric drill. Pre-drill a series of holes into the brickwork with a masonry drill bit to make the router's work that bit easier and nail a length of batten against one of the marked lines to act as a guide and ensure your router works on a straight line. You can fill in these batten-fixing holes at the same time as you cover in the channel.

along one side of the cable and then feed the cable – sticky side inwards – into the channel. The adhesive will ensure the cable remains in place while you fill in the channel. Make sure the adhesive is one that will not react to PVC.

This you should do with a plaster filler. Smooth the surface of the new plaster as best you can with the filling knife and leave it to dry thoroughly. Then rub it down with medium grade glasspaper until the new plaster is really smooth and level with the existing wall surface.

There is a useful tip if you are going to paper the wall afterwards. Mark the cable run on the wall with a pencil so that if you want to check where the cable run goes at a later date, all you need do is peel away a bit of the paper to uncover the marks. Of course you will not be able to do this if you are painting the wall.

Running cable under floorboards

This method involves less damage than cutting into a wall and having to repair the plaster afterwards. With modern PVC-sheathed cable, you can quite safely run this under a timber ground floor so that it rests on the concrete sub-floor – or you can thread it between gaps in the supporting brick wall.

Even if there is any damp under the floor, it should not penetrate this type of cable, as long as the cable insulation is sound, since it is impervious to moisture. Make sure the cable lies easily and is not stretched at all. Also remember that you should not run cable through the same opening as a gas pipe in case there are leaks in either supply.

Under all timber floors, whether it is at ground level or upstairs, you will see that the boards rest on timber beams called joists. It may well be that at some stage you need to run the cable across, rather than along, these joists. If so, you will have to drill holes in the joists and feed your cable through them. But make sure you drill any holes at least 50mm (2in) below the top of each joist. This is to ensure that any nails or screws fixed into the floor later do not hit the cable or puncture it. For the same reason, never run a cable along a groove cut into the top of the joists.

When you get to the ceiling below the loft, you can either run cable along the joists or over them, provided you are not fixing a floor in the loft, if you have to cross them. If, however, you do have a floor in your loft – or decide at a later stage to lay one down, you will have to drill holes and feed the cable through each joist as before. If you decide to install loft floor insulation after laying new cables, make sure the insulation material – and this applies primarily to blanket insulation – does not stretch or trap any cables. In any case, thermal insulation should never cover the existing cables. You can run cables over the insulation; if running cable through it, the cable size may have to be increased and you should check this with a qualified electrician.

Lifting floorboards

Before you lift floorboards, examine the floor closely to see whether any of the boards have been lifted before. New nails, clean screws or marks on the edges of boards will be the obvious clues. The chances are that if certain floorboards have been lifted, this could have been to get at electrical cables running underneath – and then your search will be over. As a general rule, it is a good idea to screw lifted boards back in place – and this will provide the best clue.

To save yourself a lot of extra work, always try to lift the minimum number of floorboards. This means that if you are running cable along the joists, you only need to lift one board at each end of the cable run. Tie some string to the end of your cable and fix the other end of the string to a long piece of

When running cable under timber floorboards, your route may involve crossing the joists. In this case you will have to drill holes through each joist at least 50mm (2in) below the top of each joist. This is to ensure that anyone nailing into the joist later does not hit your cable. For this reason you should also ensure that cable runs down the middle of lengths of floorboard. When your cable run reaches the wall, make sure you cut a small notch at the end of the floorboard above the run so that it does not pinch the cable when fixed back in place.

batten. Feed this through to the other exposed board and pull the string through until the cable appears.

If you have to run the cable through joists, try to plan the run so that you only have to lift boards – hopefully just one or two – in a straight line. Remember here that the cable should run through holes drilled 50mm (2in) below the top of each joist in the centre of the floorboard to avoid possible damage from nails or screws.

Before you attempt to lift any floorboards, check to see whether they are tongued and grooved. To do this, slide a thin blade of a knife either side of the board to be lifted. If the blade hits an obstruction, then the board is tongued and you will have to cut through this to release it. Cut through on either side of the board with a tenon saw held at a shallow angle. This should prevent you cutting through any existing cable or piping underneath.

Start lifting from a convenient end by inserting a bolster or wide-bladed cold chisel and levering up the board. When there is room, slip a long cold chisel or steel rod under the board and tap this along the board, lifting it up as you go. You may have to use a lot of brute force at the other end of the board if this is under a skirting board. But be careful not to damage the skirting, which may otherwise have to be removed.

If there is not a convenient end of board at which to start lifting, you will have to cut across the board in the centre of a joist (indicated by the position of the nails or screws). First remove any screws or punch down nails well below the surface. Drill a few small holes at an angle so that you can insert a pad saw to start the cut across the board. Once you have cut right across, you can proceed to lift the board as before. The reason you should cut through the board at an angle is that when you replace the board you can fix through both angled sections of the cut.

When replacing the boards after making your electrical connections, fix them into place with 50mm (2in) long No. 8 or No. 10 countersunk screws. This will make lifting much easier if you have to work on that part of the circuit again.

Having replaced lifted boards, you may find there is a gap between the boards. You can make good – and prevent draughts – by using a wood filler or papier mâché.

If you are running cable under floorboards, you will have to lift the relevant boards first. The first job is to check whether the boards are tongued and grooved, since if they are, the tongue will have to be cut before they can be lifted. Slide a thin bladed knife into the crack; if it hits an obstruction, then you've found a tongue and you will have to cut carefully through this all down its length. Use a tenon saw for this and work with the blade at a shallow angle to avoid possible damage to any existing wiring or piping underneath.

To lift a floorboard, select a convenient end and check whether the board is nailed or screwed. Take out any screws with a screwdriver along the whole length of the board. If you cannot lift the end nails, drive them right through the bottom of the board with a hammer and nail punch. Insert a couple of bolster chisels (or suitable levers) at either side and carefully lift up the end of the board making sure you do not damage the edges of the adjoining boards.

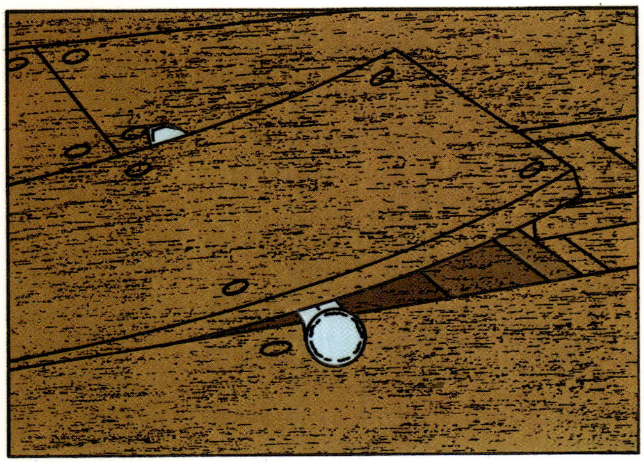

Having lifted the end, slide a long cold chisel (or a piece of steel rod or small diameter piping) under the board and work it along until the whole board has lifted clear. Remove the other nails as you go.

If you cannot find a convenient end to lift, you will have to cut through the middle of a board. Do this where the board crosses a joist to make the re-fixing easier. The position of the joists will be indicated by the lines of nails or screws in each board. Remove the screws – or sink the nails into the joist as before – and drill a few holes in the board from the centre at an angle of about 45°. This will enable you to insert the blade of a padsaw, which you should use at the same angle across the width of the board so that the cut misses the edge of the joist. When you come to re-fix the board, your nails or screws will go through both ends of board.

Running cable inside cavities

It is possible to run cable between the two leaves that form the outer cavity wall of many houses, although in practice this is best done as the wall is being built – should you ever get the opportunity.

Of course you can drill holes or remove bricks in the inner leaf and feed the cable through, but you should never do this if you have already got cavity wall insulation. The reason is that the insulation does its job on the cable as well and prevents heat from radiating away from the conductors. The result is that the cable overheats. In any case, you will find it impossible to drop the cable down through this insulation.

If you do ever run cable through thermal insulation, you may need to increase the size of the cable to prevent it overheating. This of course also applies in the loft, where any cable should be fixed to the joists above the insulation – not buried underneath.

You will find the easiest access to the cavity is from the loft and the best method here is to drop a line down the cavity with a suitably heavy weight attached to the bottom. Tie the top end of the line to your new cable, feed the weight through the hole you have made in the wall and pull the line through carefully until the cable appears. This hole will have to be large enough for you to locate and get hold of the weight – and it may even require removing a whole brick. You will probably find, too, that you are frustrated by the obstruction caused from wall ties, ends of joists, pieces of cement, etc. inside the cavity as you try to feed the cable down it.

The same principle applies with partition walls, although here the only restrictions are the cross battens. Make large enough holes where required to feed the cable through – using the weighted line as before to lower the cable.

Running cable down a cavity wall is a fairly tricky operation, since obstructions such as wall ties and sometimes the ends of floor joists may interrupt the route – and you will not be able to see these. Having made access holes at the top and bottom of the run, tie a suitable weight, such as a cold chisel, onto one end of the cable and feed it carefully down the cavity. Make sure it is tied tightly, since if it gets caught it could become detached from the cable as you try to pull it free. When it reaches the bottom opening you can pull it, with the end of the cable, back into the room. You may find that with a short run a length of strong thick fencing wire will do the job equally well, and it has the advantage that you can push it down at an angle where necessary to clear any obstruction you come up against.

Access through a partition wall is relatively simple, since you can easily knock a small hole in the plasterboard and feed in your length of cable. Make a hole at the bottom through which you can pull out the cable, but make sure this hole is not larger than the fitting to be wired up or you will have to make good the hole before you can install the fitting. Again, you should weight the end of the cable to help it fall down the cavity to the opening at the bottom.

Fixing cable along the wall

The easiest method of running cable is to fix it to the surface of the wall, although the overall effect will look rather untidy. You can either use metal clips or the more modern plastic clips with hardened pins; these can be driven into a brick wall. Make sure that the pins are long enough to grip the wall firmly. They should enter the brickwork and not just the plaster.

When running cable along the surface of a wall, use either metal or plastic clips. The latter have hardened pins which will penetrate brickwork. Make sure when you nail them at intervals along the cable run that they do not pierce existing cable in the wall. Ensure that the clips are the right size for the cable; they should fit tightly over it. To prevent sagging on long horizontal runs, you can secure the cable to the wall at intervals with blobs of contact adhesive.

Mark the cable run along or up the wall with a straight-edge and fix the cable with the clips one at a time as you go. Your fixing points should never be more than 250mm (10in) apart on a horizontal run or 400mm (16in) on a vertical run. It is much better to space the clips closer than this to ensure the cable is properly secure and does not sag in between the fixing points.

To help keep the cable in position while you clip it onto the wall – and to ensure none of it starts sagging – apply non-reacting contact adhesive at regular intervals along the back of the cable to hold it firmly in position (see pages 91–93).

One word of warning. Never run exposed cable along the top or bottom of a skirting board. At that level, it is vulnerable to furniture that is being moved about, vacuum cleaners and possibly feet, too. If you want to run your cable at this level, you can buy special hollow plastic skirting board through which you can run lengths of cable safely – or PVC mini-trunking which comes with fittings.

Feeding cable through conduit

To save feeding cable through walls or cutting channels into walls, you can run cable along lengths of conduit, which you fix to the wall. Traditionally these were made of metal for use with a single core cable. Nowadays strong plastic conduit is also available. The conduit is fixed to the wall by means of special clips or saddles.

Incidentally, you can use conduit to run cables along the sides of joists as well for added protection. If you use steel conduit, make sure you fix PVC or rubber bushes at either end of the conduit to prevent the possibility of the cable being damaged on the metal as you feed it through.

You can get special metal or plastic skirting through which cable can be fed in a special channel. This is probably the easiest method of running cable, since it requires the minimum amount of preparation work and little or no making good afterwards. You simply replace the existing skirting with the cable-carrying type, which is secured to the wall with special clips or saddles. When using metal skirting to carry cable, make sure you fit a rubber bush to each end of the channel to prevent the cable chaffing. The cable should be stiff enough to be fed through the channel. Alternatively thread strong cord through the channels before you fit the skirting, tie one end of the cable to the cord and pull the cord through.

Wall-mounting boxes

Whenever an electrical fitting is fixed to the wall, you will need to install a wall-mounting box, through which the cables are fed before being connected to the terminals on the back of the switch plate, which is itself fixed onto the box. The switch plate could be that of a light, a socket or a fused connection unit.

The boxes are made from galvanised steel or plastic and are fitted with 'knock-out' plugs through which lengths of cable can be fed. These plugs are positioned in the back and sides of the box so that you can knock out a hole for your cable wherever convenient in the box.

The two types of box available are a deep version, which is for use with a flush-mounted fitting and is recessed into the wall, and a shallow version, which is used with light switches and wall-mounted socket outlets. The boxes have fixing holes through which screws are fitted into plugged holes in the wall. And each box is designed to take the retaining screws that hold the switch plate in position.

When installing a wall-mounting box for a new fitting, first work out the most suitable position to avoid existing cable runs (see pages 90–91). Then hold the box to the wall and mark its outline and the channel for the cable run (see pages 91–93). Extend the four sides of the box outline slightly to allow space for the grommets, which are fitted in the cable entry holes. Score round the marked outline with a sharp cutting knife to help prevent the surrounding plaster cracking as you chip away the hole.

Installing wall-mounting boxes

When installing a wall-mounting box, you should already have worked out where you want to position the electrical fitting in question when you planned your cable run. It is worth remembering a few points here. For example, wall socket outlets should be at least 150mm (6in) up from the floor to avoid the possibility of damage from things like vacuum cleaners or clumsy feet. Check on the safety points already discussed (see pages 13–27) and bear in mind particularly the restrictions listed for kitchens and bathrooms.

The first job is to mark out the position of the box on the wall. Hold the box where you want the fitting to be and trace the outline onto the wall. Make sure the box is horizontal by laying a small spirit level on top of the box or by checking that the distance from the box to the floor is the same on both sides.

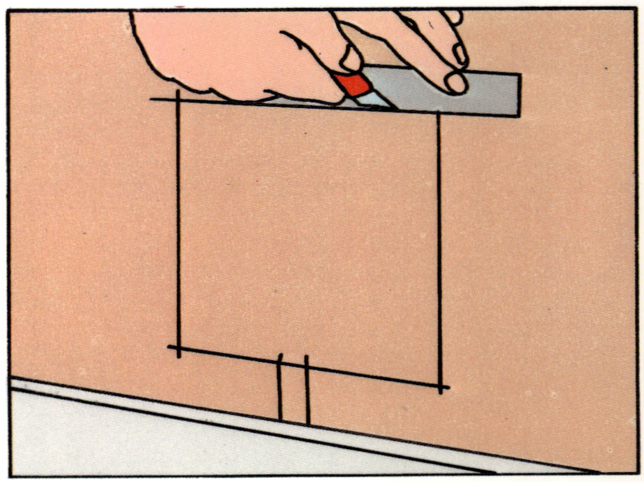

With a brick bolster and club hammer carefully remove the plaster from the marked area.

Measure the depth of the wall-mounting box and mark this distance on the drill bit with a piece of sticky tape to ensure that you drill to the correct depth. Then drill a series of holes across the area for the box into the brickwork. Chip away the brickwork to the depth of the holes, testing at regular intervals until the box fits. You will find that with breeze or similar building blocks you will not have to drill holes all over – just enough to mark the depth of the hole. Clean the hole out, put in the box and mark the fixing holes, then remove the box and drill and plug these holes.

Having completed your cable run and sunk the cable into its channel, fit a grommet in the cable-entry hole, feed in the end of the cable and insert the wall-mounting box. Finally screw the box into place before connecting up the cable conductors.

Remove the box and score carefully around the marked outline with a sharp cutting knife. This will help prevent the plaster around the box cracking as you remove the plaster inside the box area.

As a guide to ensure you remove exactly the right depth of plaster and, if necessary, brickwork, make a hole in each corner of the box area with a masonry drill bit attached to an electric drill. Make each hole the same depth as the box. The easiest way to do this is to measure this depth from the tip of the drill bit and wrap a strip of sticky tape round it. All you then have to do is to drive the bit into the wall until you reach the tape, then stop.

The depth of the hole will of course depend on the type of box you are using. With some shallower fittings with the thinner boxes, you may only have to remove the plaster to recess the box. With flush-mounted fittings which have deeper boxes, you will have to remove some of the brickwork as well.

Remove the necessary amount of plaster and brickwork with a bolster chisel and club hammer. When you reach the brickwork, chip away small pieces at a time and do not attempt to remove too much at once. You will soon find what a tough material brick is when you start working. One tip here is to drill a series of holes in the brickwork to make the chipping-out that much easier.

When you have chipped away to the depth of the four holes already drilled, place the box in the hole to check you have cut away the right amount of wall. Clean out the hole and remove all debris to ensure you have a snug fit. Put the box back into the cut-out area and mark through the fixing holes onto the wall behind. Remove the box and drill holes at these points with a masonry drill bit attached to an electric drill. Plug the holes at these points; these will then be ready to take the box-fixing screws.

Check to see where your cable will run into the box and knock out the relevant plugs in the box. You will find these tap out quite easily with an old chisel blade or a small cold chisel. Do not forget to fix rubber grommets into the knocked-out holes, otherwise the cable will rub against the cut metal and may get damaged.

Before you finally secure the wall-mounting box, feed the cables into it through the holes, then insert the box into the wall and secure it with the fixing screws into the pre-drilled holes. Before you make your cable connections and screw on the switch plate, make good the area around the box with plaster filler. You are bound to have a few gaps around the box and by filling them in you will achieve a really neat finish. Smooth the surface of the filler as best you can with the filling knife, leave it to dry and then give it a final rub down with medium grade glasspaper.

Securing fittings to partition walls

Fixing electrical fittings to partition walls poses an additional problem, since you cannot drill and plug holes into plasterboard in quite the same way as you can into plaster and brick. Special wall-mounting boxes are available to overcome this problem – and are specially designed to grip the plasterboard. It is, of course, important here to cut the correct size hole to take the box, since you will not be able to make good with filling plaster as easily as you can with a solid wall.

Put the box against the plasterboard in the position you want your electrical fitting and mark round it with a pencil. Score round the area with a sharp cutting knife and then drill a few holes to enable you to get an old hacksaw blade into the plasterboard. Cut out the marked area carefully. Knock out holes in the box as required, fit grommets and feed the cable through. With the wall-mounting box correctly positioned, it will be firmly clamped in place as the switch plate is fitted.

If you are fixing surface-mounted fittings, you can screw these directly onto the plasterboard with special plasterboard plugs. These come in two basic designs – anchors which expand against the plasterboard when the screw is inserted and toggles which open out when they are through the plasterboard, preventing any forward movement.

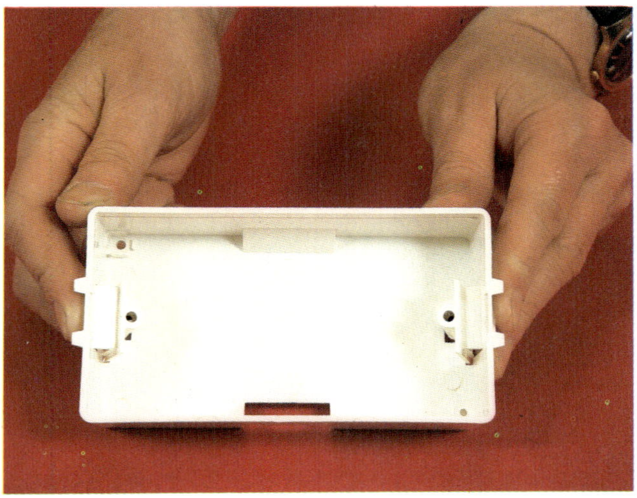

A special type of wall-mounting box is available for use in partition walls. Made in plastic or metal, this box has special lugs fitted which grip the back of the plasterboard facing as the retaining screws are tightened.

For surface-mounted fittings on plasterboard, there are special fixings available that enable you to secure the fitting. Anchors work on the principle of expanding against the plasterboard as the screw is inserted, while toggles open out after they have been fed through the plasterboard and prevent any forward movement. Always use the strongest fixings available for electrical fittings.

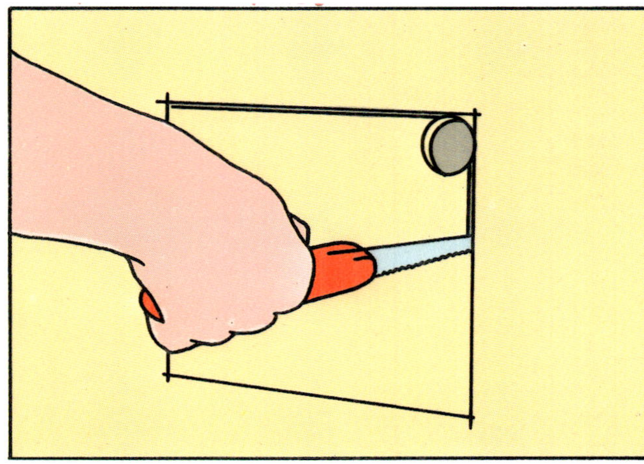

When fitting a wall-mounting box in a partition wall, it is very important to cut exactly the right size hole since the job of making good around the hole is a lot harder with plasterboard than with a solid wall. Having marked the outline of the box on the wall, make a hole large enough to take a padsaw blade and cut out the marked area with this blade. You will be less likely to damage the surrounding plasterboard if you score along the marked outline first with a sharp cutting knife.

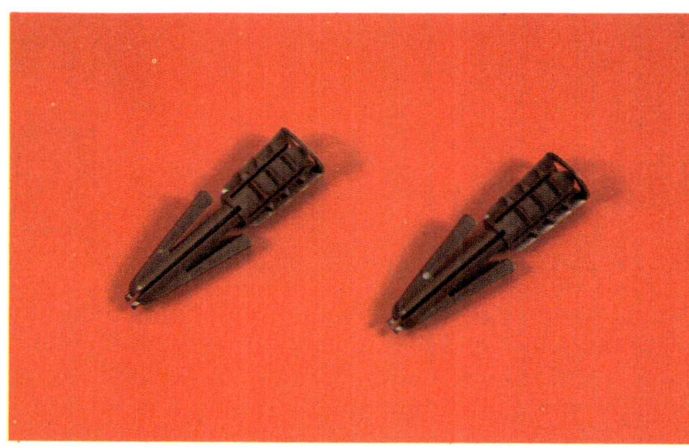

Fitting a spur to a power ring main

If you want to fit an extra socket outlet, it may be possible to add it to an existing ring main circuit. But you must check that the following conditions are observed:

1. Each spur may only feed one single or double socket outlet.
2. The total number of spur outlets on a ring main circuit must not exceed the original number of outlets.
3. The cable used must be the same size as or larger than that of the original ring circuit.

The advantage of wiring up a spur is that it can be taken from the nearest convenient ring main socket outlet. But it is vital to remember that you should never fit a spur from a socket outlet that is itself already a spur.

First decide where you want to position your new socket outlet. Then locate the nearest ring main socket outlet – one that is not already a spur.

The way to check this is quite simple. First turn off the power at the mains, then remove the switch plate from the selected outlet. There must be two conductors of each colour (red and black) feeding into the terminals on the back of the plate. If there

This simplified wiring layout shows socket outlets on a ring circuit, one of which (B) has already been used to feed a spur – and therefore cannot be used again. E is a spur and feeds another socket (F), neither of which can be used to feed another spur. A, C and D are all available for use to feed a spur. Remember that although you may have two socket outlets on a spur in your home, recent regulations recommend that only one socket outlet should be used on a spur. Ideally you should change one of the socket outlets to comply with the regulations.

is only one set of conductors, then you have chosen an outlet that is already a spur and therefore cannot be used.

If there are two sets of conductors, you now have to check the nearest socket outlets on either side of this one, since the outlet you have chosen could still be a spur that is feeding another socket outlet – hence the two sets of conductors. If you find that the two adjacent socket outlets both have two sets of conductors feeding them, then your selected socket outlet is on a ring main and is not a spur – and so can be used to feed off a spur. But if either of the adjacent socket outlets has only one set of conductors feeding it, you have chosen a spur outlet and cannot use it.

Until recently you were allowed to wire two individual outlets on a single spur, which is why you must carry out this check. If, in fact, your chosen socket outlet has three sets of conductors feeding it, then you will know a spur has already been taken from this one – and again you cannot use it. If you cannot find a convenient socket outlet to use for your spur, you will have to feed the spur direct from the ring main.

When you have located a suitable ring main socket outlet for your spur, you can proceed to wire up your new socket outlet. Having planned your new cable route and established the exact position of your new socket outlet, channel out the cable run – or adopt the appropriate techniques if you are running cable in a different way (see pages 90–99) – and fit the wall-mounting box (see pages 100–102).

Don't forget to put a rubber grommet in the hole of the new box through which your cable is to be fed – and also one in the hole you decide to knock out in the existing box, which you will have to unscrew and lever out from the wall.

Feed about 125mm (5in) of cable into the new box and then lay the cable into the prepared run to the existing socket outlet. Remember here not to fix the cable permanently until you have made your connections at either end. If you do, and you make a mistake and have to trim off more of the cable, you could run into problems.

Make sure you feed about 125mm (5in) of cable into the existing box as well. Then strip off about 100mm (4in) of the outer insulation from the cable at each end and about 15mm (⅝in) of insulation from each end of the red and black conductors (see pages 50–53). The earth conductor will be bare and you should slip a piece of green/yellow insulation sleeving over it at either end, leaving about 15mm (⅝in) exposed.

Arrange the new conductors neatly alongside the existing ones in the box – matching them colour for colour (that is red with red, black with black and green/yellow earth with green/yellow earth). Then feed the new conductors into their relevant terminals, having slackened the screws, and tighten them securely. Check that the conductors lie comfortably in the box and are not twisted or caught up. Replace the switch plate onto the box.

Then go to the new socket outlet and carry out the same procedure of connecting up the conductors to the new switch plate terminals. The one difference here is that you will have to connect a small piece of suitably sized earth wire from the earth terminal on the back of the switch plate to the earth terminal in the box. Don't forget to slip a green/yellow sleeve over this piece of earth wire. When you have checked the connections, fit on the switch plate. All that is left is to make good the decorations around the new socket outlet. Secure the cable if you have channelled it into the wall and make good this channel before redecorating (see pages 92–93).

Having selected a suitable socket outlet from which to feed your spur, you will need to prepare your cable route (see pages 91–93) and make a hole for the wall-mounting box for your new socket outlet (see pages 82–83). You should, of course, have already switched off the power at the consumer unit or removed the fuse in the relevant circuit. To enable you to make the necessary connections in the existing socket outlet, you will have to take off the switch plate, undo the conductors and remove the wall-mounting box. Knock out another cable-entry hole in the box, fit a grommet and feed the end of the new cable into the box. You can then replace this box.

Having made the hole for your new wall-mounting box, knock out a cable-entry hole in the box, fit a grommet and feed the other end of the new cable through it. Fix the new box into the wall. Until you have made the connections, it is advisable not to bury the cable (should you be using this method) in case you make a mistake or the length of cable has to be adjusted. Just stick the cable lightly in the channel with a little contact adhesive.

When you have checked the work so far and made sure that your cable reaches both switch plates to enable you to connect up, you can then wire in the new socket outlet. Make the connections in the existing socket outlet first, matching up the three red conductors and fitting them to the live terminal; the three black conductors go to the neutral terminal, and the three bare conductors (fitted with green/yellow plastic sleeves) connect to the earth terminal. At the other end of the new cable, wire up the one set of conductors to the equivalent terminals in the new socket outlet. Fit a short length of earth connector covered with a green/yellow plastic sleeve from the earth terminal on the fitting to the earth terminal in the wall-mounting box. Check all your connections are secure, then replace both switch plates and restore the power to the circuit.

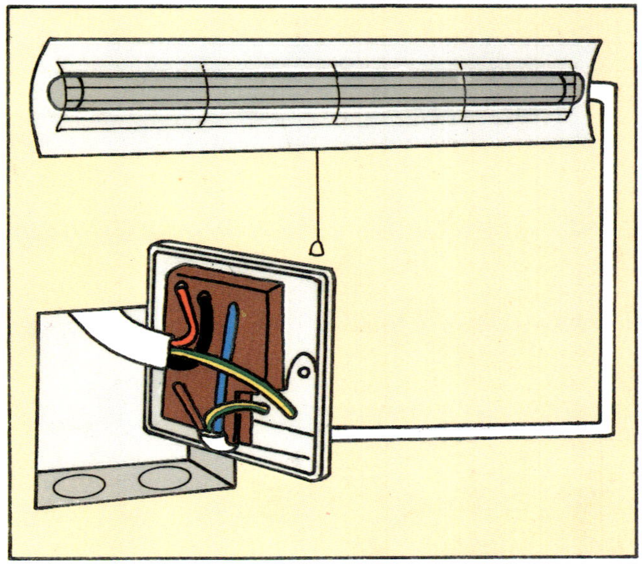

When fitting a fixed appliance as a spur from a socket outlet, you should run the cable through a fused connection unit. To wire the unit up to the socket outlet, follow the procedure as for a socket outlet on a spur (see pages 77–79). The connections in the unit are slightly different, however. On the face plate of the unit you will see two sets of terminals – one marked IN and the other OUT – as well as the earth terminal. The live and neutral conductors in the cable from the socket outlet must be connected to the IN terminals. The OUT terminals take the live and neutral conductors in the flex to the fixed appliance. The earth conductors from the cable and the flex share the earth terminal. Having made the necessary connections, check on the fuse in the unit. This should be rated at 3amp for an appliance with a load of up to 700 watts and 13 amp for an appliance of up to 3kW. Any appliance with a loading of more than 3kW must be wired up on its own circuit direct from the consumer unit and carrying its own main fuse.

Fitting a fixed appliance as a spur

You can fit a fixed appliance, such as a bathroom heater, as a spur from an existing ring main socket outlet in much the same way as a new socket outlet. Instead of fitting a socket outlet switch plate to the new wall-mounting box, however, you fix a cable termination point over the new box.

If the appliance is fed by a flexible cord – such as on a wall heater – you will have to fix a fused connection unit to the new box and feed the flex from this to the appliance. One point to note here is that the terminals on the unit will be marked IN and OUT. This means that the spur cable conductors should be connected to the IN terminals and the flex conductors to the OUT terminals. And make sure you tighten the cord-grip screws in the fused connection unit when the wiring up is complete.

Fitting a spur direct from a ring main circuit

You may sometimes find that there is not a conveniently placed socket outlet from which to feed a spur to the new socket outlet – or that the nearest socket outlets are already on a spur or feeding a spur. In this case the easiest way to run cable to your new socket outlet is to take it direct from the ring main cable.

To do this you will need to fit a junction box at a convenient position in the ring main cable run.

The first job is to locate a suitable length of ring main cable and ensure that it is not already part of a spur. Use the spur check on the adjacent socket outlets (see pages 104–105).

You can fix the junction box under the floor onto a suitable joist, having located the correct cable by lifting the floorboards (see pages 94–96).

Having established the best position for the junction box, unscrew the switch plate and fix the

If there is no suitable socket outlet nearby from which to run a spur, you can fit a junction box into the ring circuit. Select a suitable position for the junction box – either on the wall or fitted to a joist or between joists (see pages 110–111) under the floorboards. Unscrew the box cover and fit the box with screws provided. You will have to chip out three holes in the side of the box to take the two ends of the ring circuit cable (which you will have to cut) and the cable for the spur. Do this carefully with the blade of an old screwdriver or chisel. Prepare the ends of the cables and connect the three sets of conductors to their relevant terminals – red to live, black to neutral and green/yellow to earth. Secure the connections and make sure the conductors lie comfortably in the box before screwing back the cover.

back of the box to the wall or joist with the screws provided. With wall fittings, you will have to drill holes and plug them. (For partition walls see pages 102–103.)

If you are fitting the box to timber, first drill pilot holes to take the screws. You will have to chip out three holes in the side of the box base with an old screwdriver, into which you will feed the two cut ends of the ring main cable and the new spur cable. Make sure there are no sharp edges by filing the holes smooth. Now you can prepare the ring main cable and make all the necessary connections.

To do this, strip back a sufficient amount of the outer insulation from the ring main cable – at least 75mm (3in) – and cut through all the conductors. Strip off 15mm (5/8in) of insulation from each of the conductors at the two exposed ends of cable. Since you have three sets of conductors, two for the ring main cable and one for the spur cable, connect the three black conductors together, the three red conductors together and the three earth conductors together into different terminals in the junction box. Tighten up the connections and make sure all the conductors lie comfortably in the box before replacing the box cover.

To avoid cutting cable, it is much better, however, to use the most recent type of junction box. This is designed to allow cable to be run through the box without it being cut. All you need do is strip back a section of the insulation to expose the conductors and lay it in the terminals.

Adding a light controlled by an existing switch

You may decide you want to install an extra light in the room, but do not want to go to the trouble of having it independently switched. In this case, you can make the new fitting and connect it with the existing light switch.

First decide where you want to position the new light on the ceiling. Having established this, you will have to lift the floorboards in the room immediately above it and those above the existing ceiling rose to which your new rose will be connected.

To work out exactly which floorboards need lifting, you will have to measure both light positions on the ceiling – the nearest distance from two adjacent walls – and use these measurements from the same walls in the room above.

Having lifted the relevant floorboards (see pages 94–96), make a hole down through the ceiling large enough to take the cable for the new rose – approximately 25mm (1in). The same size hole should be drilled in a piece of 100 × 25mm (4 × 1in) timber which you must fix between the joists (see pages 110–111) and into which the new ceiling rose can then be fitted with the screws provided.

Thread a two-core and earth 1sq mm cable down through the holes in the piece of timber, the ceiling and the base of the ceiling rose and strip back about 75mm (3in) of the outer insulation and about 15mm (5/8in) of the insulation on the red and black conductors. The earth conductor will of course be bare and you should put a piece of green/yellow sleeving onto this, leaving the end exposed.

Connect the earth conductor to the earth terminal on the ceiling rose. Then connect the black conductor to the middle of the three N terminals and the red conductor to the inner of the two switch terminals.

At this stage you should prepare the lampholder flex. First cut it to the desired length, depending on how far from the ceiling you want your new light to hang. Bare the ends of the flex 15mm (5/8in) and, taking one end, connect the brown conductor to the outer of the two switch terminals on the ceiling rose and blue conductor to one of the spare N terminals. Slide the ceiling rose cover over the free end of flex and screw it to the rose base.

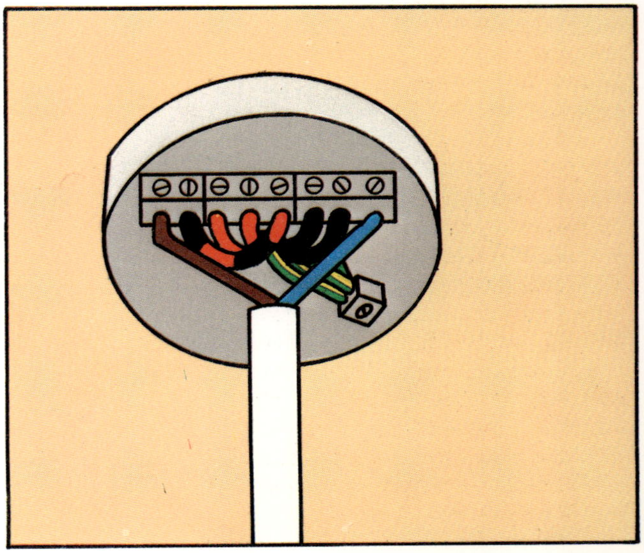

To add a ceiling light wired up to an existing light switch, you will first have to install the light fitting. Select a suitable position on the ceiling, then lift the relevant board from the floor in the room above. The ceiling rose will have to be mounted between joists and this will involve fixing a wooden mounting block between the joists (see page 64). Before you fix this piece of wood, drill a 25mm (1in) hole through the centre; this will take the cable. When the mounting block is in place, use this hole as a guide to make a hole down through the plasterboard ceiling into the room below. Make the hole carefully to avoid damaging too much of the ceiling below.

Fix the base of the ceiling rose onto the mounting block from below the ceiling and feed the end of the cable through the hole into it. Connect up the black conductor to the middle of the three N terminals and the red conductor to the inner of the two switch terminals. The bare conductor with a green/yellow plastic sleeve fitted goes to the earth terminal.

Having prepared your new lampholder and flex (see pages 50–53, 64–65), make the connections to the new ceiling rose. One conductor should be connected to the neutral terminal and the other to the switch terminal (it does not matter which way round they go). Having made the connections, you can screw on the ceiling rose cover.

The final connection is wiring up the new ceiling rose cable to the existing ceiling rose nearby. At this stage you must switch off the power since you will be working on a 'live' circuit from now on. You will have to feed the end of the new cable down the existing hole above the original ceiling rose. Undo the ceiling rose cover and feed the new cable down through the hole. Connect the bare conductor (with a green/yellow sleeve) to the earth terminal. The black conductor is fitted to the middle of the three N terminals (which will now be shared) and the red conductor goes to the inner switch terminal, which should already carry a black conductor with a red sleeve on it. Check all your connections, screw back the rose cover and restore the power to the circuit.

Remove the top of the lampholder and thread this over the flex. It is a good idea to tape it out of the way on the flex to stop it slipping off while you connect up the lampholder. Connect the two conductors to the terminals on the lampholder (it doesn't matter which) and then screw on the top of the lampholder.

All this work can be done prior to switching off the power at the mains, since you have not yet had to make a connection to the existing circuit. But now you must turn off the power and test to ensure the circuit is not live.

Having switched off the power, remove the cover from the existing ceiling rose. Run your new length of cable to the existing rose and feed it through the hole in the ceiling into the rose. Strip back the insulation on the cable as before and bare the two insulated conductors. Do not forget to put a green/yellow sleeve on the bare earth conductor and then connect this to the earth terminal.

Connect the black conductor to the middle on the three N terminals together with the conductor that is already there and connect the red conductor to the inner switch terminal, which should already have a black conductor fitted with a red sleeve.

Having checked the wiring to make sure you have made the correct connections, and tested the circuit, screw on the ceiling rose cover and switch the power back on.

Adding a light controlled by its own switch

When you need to install an extra light but want to be able to control it separately from the existing light, you will need to wire it to its own switch. However you will still need to connect the new ceiling rose to the existing one in order to feed through the power.

Fit the new ceiling rose as described above. The difference now is in the connections you make to

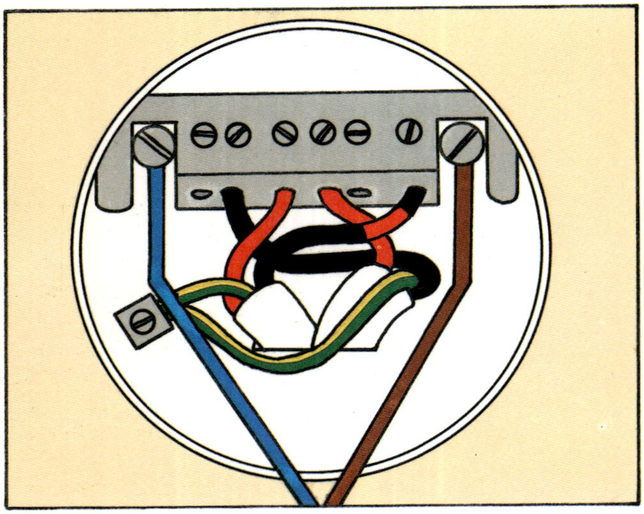

When adding a light that you want to be controlled by its own switch, you can do nearly all the installation work without switching off the power. Only when you come to connect up to the existing ceiling rose will this be necessary. Plan the position of the new ceiling rose and fit this as before (see pages 110–111). Prepare the cable run to the switch and install the wall-mounting box for the switch (see pages 66–72). Then you can make the connections to the new ceiling rose. With the new cable that will feed from the existing ceiling rose to the new one, the black conductor should be connected to the middle of the three N terminals and the red conductor to the middle of the three L terminals. With the cable that feeds the new switch, the red conductor should be connected to one of the remaining two live terminals and the black conductor to the inner of the two switch terminals; this conductor should carry a red sleeve to indicate it is switched live. Both earth conductors (with green/yellow sleeves) are connected to the earth terminal. The connections for the lampholder flex are as before (see pages 72–73).

When making the connections to the switch, ensure that the red conductor is fitted to the common terminal on the switch plate and the black conductor (with red sleeve) to the L2 terminal. The earth conductor (with a green/yellow sleeve) is fitted to the earth terminal in the wall-mounting box. Check the connections and fit on the switch plate making sure the conductors fit neatly inside the wall-mounting box. Secure the switch plate with the two screws provided.

the terminals. In the existing rose the black in the cable from the new rose must be connected to the middle of the three N terminals and the red conductor to the middle of the three L terminals. The earth connections are as mentioned above. In the new rose the black conductor is connected to the middle of the three N terminals and the red conductor to the middle of the three L terminals.

You will of course need to feed down into the new ceiling rose an additional two-core and earth

Having made all the connections in the new ceiling rose and switch, turn off the power and connect the end of the new cable to the existing ceiling rose nearby. The connections here should be as follows: the black conductor to the middle of the three N terminals and the red to the middle of the three L terminals. The earth conductor goes to the earth terminal. Having checked all the connections, replace the cover on the existing ceiling rose and restore the power to the circuit.

lsq mm cable, which will be the new switch cable. With this cable, the red conductor should be fitted to the same terminal as the red conductor from the existing ceiling rose and the black conductor to the inner of the two switch connectors. This black conductor should have a short red sleeve slipped over it. The earth conductor is connected as before. The connections for the lampholder flex are also the same as before.

Having connected this end of the switch cable, you will have to work out the position of the switch and a suitable run for the cable to do it (see pages 90–91). Points to remember are the rubber grommet in the knock-out hole in the new wall-mounting box for the light switch and sufficient allowance of cable length to enable you to make the connections easily.

Now strip back the insulation on the switch end of the cable as before and prepare the conductors. Do not forget the green/yellow sleeve on the bare earth. Connect the red conductor to the common terminal on the back of the switch plate and the black conductor to the terminal marked L2. This conductor should have a short red sleeve fitted over. Slip a piece of green/yellow sleeve over the bare earth wire and connect this to the earth terminal in the wall-mounting box.

All that is left is to screw on the switch plate to the box and turn on the power at the mains.

Wiring a light from a junction box

It may well be that you want to install an extra light but it is not convenient or possible to feed it from an existing ceiling rose. Equally you may want to install a light where there has not been one before and therefore there is no existing ceiling rose.

Here the same principle applies as for wiring a socket outlet from the ring main. You will have to connect the new ceiling rose and switch to a conveniently positioned junction box in the lighting circuit or – if one does not exist – install a junction box in this existing circuit. Putting in a junction box here involves the same techniques as for a ring main circuit (see pages 108–109). The fitting and connection of the new ceiling rose and switch are as already described, but the connections for the new cable from the ceiling rose to the junction box are as follows.

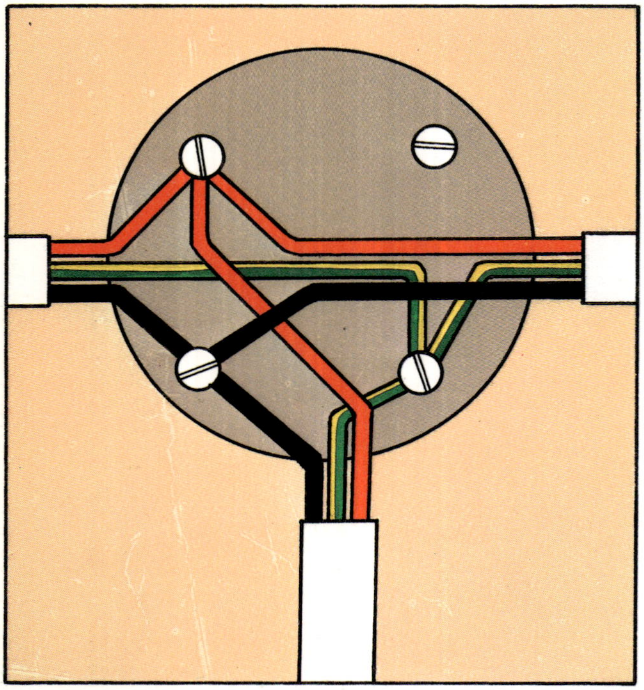

As with the power circuit, you may find there is not a convenient ceiling rose from which to feed a new ceiling rose and light. In this case you can fit a junction box in a convenient place on the lighting circuit to take your new light from that. First, fit the new ceiling rose, light and switch as already described (see pages 110–111), having decided on the siting of the junction box. Take the new ceiling rose cable to this position, turn off the power and install the junction box (see page 61). The wiring of the ceiling rose cable to the junction box is as follows: the red conductor to the terminal with the other red conductors already connected – and the black conductor to the terminal with the black conductors already connected. The earth conductor connects to the shared earth terminal.

Wire the new cable – from the ceiling rose to the junction box – with the red conductor connected to the terminal having two or more red conductors already connected to it – and similarly with the black conductor to the terminal with other black conductors. Connect up earth conductors together as well.

Fitting wall lights

The procedure for fitting and connecting wall lights is similar to the method of wiring in additional lights as already described. However, instead of having lampholders and flex to a ceiling rose, wall lights are normally fitted onto recessed wall-mounting boxes.

But remember, just because they are fixed to the wall, never try to wire them up to a power circuit unless you wire them through a fused spur connection. They would normally be wired to the lighting circuit.

Controlling an existing light with an extra switch

You may find you want to control an existing light from more than one switch – in, for example, a room with two entrances or where you want to operate a hall light from the landing or vice-versa. Fortunately the work involved does not include any modifications to the light fitting itself.

First you must check to see if the existing switch is a two-way type. Switch off the power at the mains and unscrew and lift off the switch plate. If it is a two-way switch, you will see three terminals – one labelled common (or C) and the other two L1 and L2. If the unit contains two or more switches it will automatically be two-way. If there are only two terminals, then it is a one-way switch and you will have to replace it with a two-way type (see pages 68–72).

To connect the extra switch, first decide where you want it and then fit the wall-mounting box for the new switch and prepare the cable run (see pages 90–92). You must use a three-core and earth 1sq mm cable for this job – that is, a total of four conductors, which will be coloured red, yellow and blue, plus the bare earth. Prepare the ends of the cable as normal and slip a green/yellow sleeve over the bare earth conductor. Connect this conductor to the earth terminal in each of the wall-mounting boxes.

In the existing switch you will see that the original black and red conductors are connected to terminals L1 and L2 – and it does not matter which conductor goes to which. When wiring up the new switch cable, connect the red conductor to the common terminal in both switches, the yellow conductor to the L1 terminal in both switches and the blue conductor to the L2 terminal in both switches.

As always, make sure the conductors are sitting neatly in the boxes, check all connections and screw the switch plates back on to their respective boxes. Finally turn the power back on.

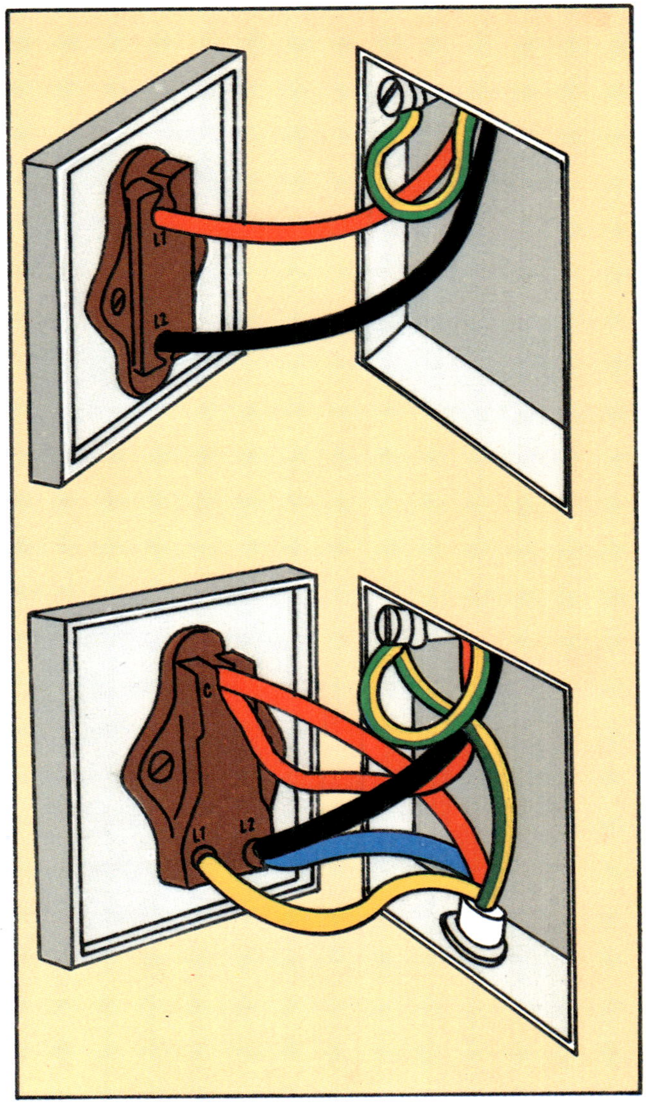

If you want to control an existing light with a second switch, you must first check that the existing switch is two-way; if not, you will have to fit a two-way switch in place of the existing one-way type. The two-way type is necessary to make the connections to the new switch. The terminal layout on these switches does vary from make to make, but the labelling is always the same. The cable you must use to connect the new switch to the existing one is three-core and earth and the wiring is as follows: the yellow conductor to L1, the blue conductor to L2 and the red conductor to Common. The bare conductor (with the green/yellow sleeve) is connected to earth in the normal way.

Replacing an old wall-mounted switch with a flush switch

In older properties you may still find the traditional light switch mounted on a wooden plinth. It is relatively straightforward to remove this fitting and replace it with a modern flush-fitted switch.

First, as always, turn off at the mains. Remove the switch cover and unscrew the terminals, then unscrew the switch from its plinth and lift it off. The plinth itself will be screwed to the wall – and this should also be removed. This will expose the cable in the wall and you should check this carefully to make sure it is not worn or damaged. If it is, you will have to replace the whole cable (see pages 90–99).

Position your wall-mounting box, which ideally should be about 15mm (5/8in) deep, over the existing wiring – ensuring that the existing cable will feed comfortably through it to the terminals on the new switch plate. Then fit the box into the wall (see pages 100–102). When you have made a hole in the wall large enough to take the box, knock out a hole through which to feed the cable into the box and fit a grommet into it. Feed in the cable and secure the box in position (see pages 100–102). When fitting the box, take great care not to damage the existing cable as you chip away the hole.

Having fitted the box, connect up the red conductor to the common terminal on the switch plate and the black conductor to the L2 terminal. If there is an earth conductor, this should be connected to the earth terminal in the wall-mounting box. When you have checked the connections, screw on the switch plate.

Replacing a pendant light with a striplight

Particularly in older homes, you may find a single pendant light in, for example, a kitchen, where a striplight would be much more efficient and practical. Equally you may want to convert a spare room into a work room and for that reason want to install a more powerful and diffused light. In this case you can remove the pendant light and fix a striplight in its place.

Switch off at the mains and then remove the existing ceiling rose cover. Disconnect and remove the flex and lampholder from the fitting. If there are only two conductors feeding the ceiling rose, you can disconnect these and remove the ceiling rose.

With modern ceiling roses the wiring is more complex. Since fluorescent light fittings do not make provision for the various conductor terminals in this type of fitting, you will have to use a suitably sized terminal strip to wire up the new light fitting.

With the modern rose fitting, you will see there are three red conductors in the centre, all connected together. You will have to connect all these to one pair of terminals in the new strip. Connect the two black conductors together in another terminal on the strip, leaving the other end of the terminal strip free. The black conductor which may have a red sleeve over it (that is, 'switched live') should be connected to another terminal, leaving the other end of the terminal free. The green or green/yellow terminal conductors should be connected together in another pair of terminals.

Having connected up the existing cable, you now need to wire in the new flex which will connect up the fluorescent light fitting. Using a length of 1.0sq mm three-core PVC-sheathed round flex, connect the three conductors – red to brown, black to blue and green/yellow to green/yellow – into the three free terminals on the terminal block. Having made all these connections, you can discard the original ceiling rose.

It is very important to ensure the fluorescent light fitting is securely fixed to the ceiling. Ideally it should be screwed into a convenient joist above –

and this should be borne in mind before you wire up the terminal block in case you want to move the cable across the ceiling to a new position (see pages 93–96).

If the ideal position for the light fitting does not coincide with a joist, you will have to fix a piece of wood between two joists and screw the fitting into that (see page 64). The mounting for a fluorescent tube is similar to a wall-mounting box – though of course much longer – and will have knock-out holes through which the cable can be fed. Don't forget to put in a grommet to prevent the cable fraying against the edges of the hole.

Connect the brown conductor to the L terminal in the tube mounting and the blue conductor to the N terminal. The green/yellow earth conductor is connected to the earth terminal. If there is no earth terminal at the ceiling rose, this circuit will need rewiring.

When you have checked the connections and ensured they are tightened, put on the striplight cover and insert the tube.

When wiring up a striplight in place of a pendant light from the existing ceiling rose, you will have to replace the existing terminal arrangement with a four-way terminal block. Having removed the lampholder flex, you will be left with three sets of conductors – two from the lighting circuit cables and one from the switch cable. Connect the two black conductors from the lighting circuit cables to one pair of terminals on the strip. The black conductor with a red sleeve (the switched live conductor from the switch cable) should be fitted to another terminal, leaving the other terminal of the pair free. The three red conductors should be connected to another pair of terminals. Connect the three earth conductors to the fourth remaining pair of terminals. Now wire up the flex from the striplight, making the following connections: the brown conductor to the pair of terminals in which the switched live conductor from the switch is connected, the blue conductor to the same pair of terminals as the two black conductors from the lighting circuit cables and the green/yellow conductor to the pair of terminals already carrying the other earth conductors. Because more than one conductor is being fitted to individual terminals, make sure that the connections are properly secure.

INDEX

Figures in italics refer to illustrations